Deploying HTML5

Aditya Yadav

Copyright

Deploying HTML5

Copyright © 2010 by Aditya Yadav

ISBN-13: 978-1-451-58954-2

Trademarked names may appear in this book. Rather than use a trademark symbol with every occurrence of a trademarked name, we use the names only in an editorial fashion and to the benefit of the trademark owner, with no intention of infringement of the trademark.

To Baby Alisha Who Has Made Me Realize How Beautiful Life Can Be

Contents

Foreword

Over the years I have worked with organizations that were never on the cutting edge of technology. The reasons for which were partly the risk involved, partly the knowledge of their leading practitioners, the ambiguity around cutting edge technologies as they evolve, lack of time to follow each development, and lack of a guide they could use to quickly try out the offerings, evaluate and make decisions. This book has been an attempt to answer a lot of how's and why's around the evolving HTML 5 standard as implemented by the top 5 browsers, as of date, namely IE, Safari, Chrome, Opera and Firefox.

During my stint at my p2p startup I realized that being on this side technologists think mostly in terms of breakthroughs while businesses on the other side think mostly in terms of how it solves their problems and issues. This book takes a middle path and tries to cover both by illustrating what's involved in developing applications for the web using HTML 5. We chose ASP.NET for the little serverside code because of the free superb Visual Studio Express IDE available which is very easy to setup and use. Though with very little effort the code can be made to run off any other backend using Php, Ruby or Java. The Chapter on WebSockets uses Java to develop the WebSocket Servers.

Initiating an effort to deploy HTML 5 based applications is as much a business decision as a technical decision. I think I have been able to demonstrate to people the comprehensive features that are a part of the HTML 5 standard, though issues of vendor implementations not being complete still remain which can either leave us with the choice of using the common minimum subset of features implemented across all the top 5 browsers or we could restrict the choice of browsers to increase the feature set that we deploy. With the examples in this book the reader will be able to kickstart the evaluation of HTML 5 by trying out the examples and assessing for himself the suitability of the features for use on his project.

Technical leaders and architects will also be able to estimate the effort required in such projects and the leaders will be able to understand the risk involved in utilizing HTML 5 vis. a vis. using something like Flash or Silverlight.

Other groups which have shown extensive interest in this book are R&D, & training divisions of companies, Centers of Excellence's and product companies which work with the cutting edge of technology to capitalize on it.

Business leaders would be able to build a case for deploying HTML 5 based on the material covered in this book. While new technology is not without risks but HTML 5 is at a stage of maturity at which prototypes and internal applications can be developed without a hitch, and internet applications can be deployed by the end of the year.

I hope to see a lot more applications running off HTML 5. Over the years I have learnt that business is not about technology but it's about solutions. And even though this book is pretty techie it is meant to answer the one big question "What is the HTML 5 standard and how do we leverage it for our business" While you go through this book just sit back every once in a while and think how the information presented would help you create better solutions to business problems in your company/industry. I think I would like to look at technology through those eyes.

ADITYA YADAV

Preface

The evolution of HTML 5 is nothing new for me in terms of the experience of trying to deploy new technology as a part of applications in production. I have seen a similar evolution in the Web Application area with the evolution of Silverlight on Windows and Mac and Moonlight on the Linux platform. While there are parallels HTML 5 is an industry wide standard with major browser companies abolishing their propreitary implementation in favour of implementing the HTML 5 standard.

I'm working with companies where I have gone in and explained HTML 5 but when I turn around I see that it is forgotten and not deployed. Sometimes consultants fail to create the desired impact, or generate excitement or transfer the expertise company wide. A book like this is very handy in educating the masses about this technology. This is a practitioner's book and contains working examples of all the features of HTML 5. It allows the early adopters to taste success with the technology and once they do that they try to leverage the expertise when the situation demands.

I spent about 6-8 months giving repeat presentations to interested groups both internal and at our clients. Which finally led to the writing of this book which is intended as a single weekend crash course for engineers, architects and leaders to learn what HTML 5 is all about and how to plan, migrate, and deliver applications using it.

And that is when I came across the editors who agreed with this idea and helped me convert my rough notes into a production quality book. What you read in the following chapters are tried and tested examples which work, and you will get the source code to all of them. I hope with this book it will be the best weekend you will invest in learning HTML 5.

ADITYA YADAV

Acknowledgements

Writing this book has been an exciting journey that brought several incredible people together to support me. I would like to thank the knowledgeable reviewers for some of the best feedback during the writing of this book. The advice included which topics were most important to them and from general observations in the industry wide pilot adoptions. I would like to thank people at Thoughtworks, my former employer, who helped me make up my mind to write this book.

I took a 4 month sabbatical from work to embark on this journey which has been very fulfilling in many ways. I would like to thank my father Jai Raj Yadav who financially supported me through the sabbatical and with all the resources, travel, household, loan payments and other expenses. Leaving me free to concentrate on nothing but writing the book. I would like to thank my wife Renu for her undivided support during these 4 months. We have a 2 month old baby boy and it has been hard on Renu to leave me alone for long hours undisturbed. She always remembered to serve tea to me every 2 hours all throughout this time, with a smile, I hope I have lived upto her expectations. My 3 year old daughter The Alisha Monster attacks the computer every now and then asking me to show her Disney movies but somehow she has abstained so far. I would like to thank my brother and sister in law Amit and Kalpana, and my mother R.D. Yadav for their faith in me.

I would like to thank the editors who painstakingly proofread the book and the publishers who were all the way through this journey. It is with their help we could together convert a raw idea into a production quality book.

About this book

You will be wondering if there is a need for yet another book on HTML 5. While 6 books are available on the topic for pre-order, when published this book will be the first in the world available to practitioners for reading. I have been working on HTML 5 for the last 6-8 months and have seen browsers implement HTML 5 features in bits and pieces. During this time I have been advising my clients to look at HTML 5 as a viable option for their projects especially for enterprise systems. A lot of Internet video websites have also been testing HTML 5.

I have always been asked 'Isn't HTML 5 immature, complex and unproven', 'Isn't it supposed to take 15 years to mature like HTML 4 took 10 years?' Well the answer is most browsers will support the complete featureset by the end of 2010. And it is already April and this is a good time to get started trying out HTML 5 features and educating the engineers. HTML 5 is at a stage where it is essential for leaders and architects to understand what are the features it brings, how it can be leveraged and what benefits it brings in.

I have been working with my clients on some exciting projects involving HTML 5 and like always I decided to write this book to scale my reach in educating my clients teams and quickening adoption. The book contains examples which are proven to work and tested (successfully/unsuccessfully) on the top 5 browsers Opera, IE, Firefox, Chrome and Safari. Though we have not tested the examples on Mobile versions of these browsers we feel confident that by the time this book reaches the readers the desktop browsers that support HTML 5 features would have implemented them in their mobile versions as well.

Time upon time my clients have asked me 'tell us who can we hire to build our system with HTML 5?' 'are resources available?' 'how do our teams learn?' 'we can't have our architecture group sit through analyzing the specifications and building prototypes to evaluate HTML 5 over 3-4 months' Well the bottomline is HTML 5 is not complicated its just evolving and there is a lot of confusion and scattered articles with bits and pieces over the internet. Not many developers are out there with HTML 5 skills on their resume who can come in and instantly get started. But that doesn't mean adopters are alone in their efforts. This book was meant to quicken the analysis and learning from months to the order of days. With working examples and their full source code provided, tested in all major browsers. And all HTML 5 features comprehensively explained without any preference for any commercial products or vendors.

HTML 5 is still a draft; the effort was started in 2004 and will turn in to a recommendation for all browsers somewhere in 2010, which is this year. It is expected that soon all browser implementations will support HTML 5 which is why this book is timed for launch now. We know more or less what features will we have and more or less what their specification will be. HTML 4 took 10 years and rumour mills say that HTML 5 will need 15 years to be widely adopted. But the author believes most companies will deploy html 5 for enterprise use by the end of 2010 and for wide scale internet use by end of 2011. A lot is being discussed in the HTML 5 Working Group and WHATWG mailing lists. HTML 5 specifications will not be considered complete before two complete implementations of HTML 5 specifications. This is to make sure that the specifications are implementable by the user agent designers and usable by the programmers.

HTML 5 adoption rids systems of adhoc non-standard products and tools used earlier. If you plan to use HTML 5 or want to learn it for career reasons I would recommend you to keep this one book. You won't need anything else.

Roadmap

Prepping Up outlines all the resources that are at your disposal as you go through this book and work on HTML 5 projects.

Chapter 1 discusses the basic structure of HTML 5 documents, doctype, content types, mime types, SVG, MathML, Semantics, working with older browsers and webforms.

Chapter 2 introduces the Canvas Tag and how to draw graphics on it. Users used to Graphics on desktop applications would find it very familiar.

Chapter 3 talks about the Native Drag Drop feature available in HTML 5. Anything can be dragged and dropped into.

Chapter 4 walks the reader through Browser History manipulation features available in HTML 5.

Chapter 5 discusses HTML 5 inline editing. Which is a good read for developers interested in building browser based editors or similar applications.

Chapter 6 discusses Cross-Document Messaging which also works across domains. This allows better UI level mashups.

Chapter 7 talks about creating Offline Applications with HTML 5. It explains caching the resources on the client browser and also the option of Client Side SQL engine available to aide in creating Offline Applications.

Chapter 8 focuses on Audio and Video features available in HTML 5. We will be going through a couple of tools to prepare audio & video content, creating from scratch and converting them from other formats into patent free OGG formats which HTML 5 supports.

Chapter 9 talks about GeoLocation features available in HTML 5. Which is of interest to developers working on Location Aware applications.

Chapter 10 focuses on WebStorage primarily local and session storage. Some browsers support the concept of Global Storage which is not covered but should have similar specs.

Chapter 11 talks about Server Side Events and how it replaces the need for non standard adhoc mechanisms used earlier.

Chapter 12 discusses Web Workers which are native threads available for computation intensive work in a browser.

Chapter 13 covers WebSockets, we resist using commercial software and rather we build 2 servers one from scratch using Netty and another using Jetty.

Author Online

The resources for this book can be found and the author can be reached at
http://adityayadav.com. You can download the source code accompanying this
book at the above website, and also access the errata. The above website will be
accessible as long as the book is in print. Please try the individual browser
forums. If the question still remains unanswered please send it to the author
through the author's website. The author will answer the questions and also post
them on the website for everyone to see. Though this is not a commitment on the
part of the author as his contributions to the forum and email responses remain
voluntary (and unpaid).

The author has been the CTO of one of the top 25 startups in India dealing with
global scale real-time multimedia P2P products. He is also a technology and
technology strategy consultant to fortune companies; he provides leadership
coaching and architects world class engineering organizations for his clients. He
can be reached even outside the context of this book through the author's
website.

Prepping Up

For the purpose of this book we will run all the exercises on Windows XP, but Windows Vista or Windows 7 would also do. The HTML 5 specification is implemented in parts by various browsers and it will be prudent to test all features on all browsers as the technology is evolving to be able to make production applications with the knowledge of what works on which browsers and what doesn't.

Please download the latest version of the safari browser from http://www.apple.com/safari/download/ , download the latest version of Firefox browser from http://www.mozilla.com/en-US/firefox/firefox.html , download the latest version of Chrome browser from http://www.google.com/chrome , download the latest version of Internet Explorer browser from http://www.microsoft.com/nz/windows/internet-explorer/default.aspx , and download the latest Opera browser from http://www.opera.com/ . We will be developing web applications with very limited server side code but for the purpose of this book we will be using Asp.Net for the scanty server side code used which can be run using IIS or developed using Visual Studio, either the full version if you have licenses for it or the Express version which is free and can be downloaded from http://www.microsoft.com/express/Web/ . We develop some WebSocket examples in Java using JDK1.6 which you can download from http://java.sun.com/javase/downloads/index.jsp and Eclipse IDE for JEE developers from http://www.eclipse.org/downloads/ .

It will be a good time to download the Source Code accompanying this book from http://adityayadav.com, we will just be illustrating the essential pieces of the programs and not list the complete program, for which you have to refer to the

Source Code bundle. Also you will be able to create your applications with the projects in the bundle as starting points.

Basic proficiency in using Windows, an IDE for development e.g. Visual Studio Professional or Express and developing basic HTML web applications is assumed by the author. The book will not show clips of basic steps which are done even otherwise while developing web applications, we will try to illustrate only that is specific to HTML 5 development.

Chapter 1- Introduction to HTML 5

Let's us define two categories of consumers for HTML 5. First are programmers like you and me and the second are user agents aka browsers. HTML 5 defines both the specifications for HTML 5 features and provides guidelines for user agents so that the implementations across browsers are more or less uniform. While HTML 5 does away with a lot of HTML 4 Tags and Attributes and programmers are not supposed to be using them. But the user agents will continue to support them for those programmers that are still using HTML 4 or earlier specs.

The Basic Structure & HTML & XML Formats

HTML 5 defines a syntax that is compatible with HTML 4 and XHTML1. They are meant to be served with the mime type of 'text/html'. A basic HTML 5 document is outlined below.

```
<!doctype html>
<html>
 <head>
  <meta charset="UTF-8">
  <title>Example document</title>
 </head>
 <body>
  <p>Example paragraph</p>
 </body>
</html>
```

A basic XML format HTML 5 document is meant to be served with 'application/xhtml+xml' or 'application/xml'. An example is shown below.

```
<?xml version="1.0" encoding="UTF-8"?>
<html xmlns="http://www.w3.org/1999/xhtml">
 <head>
  <title>Example document</title>
 </head>
 <body>
  <p>Example paragraph</p>
```

```
</body>
</html>
```

Doctype

The doctype is to make sure that the document is rendered in standard mode in the browser. The doctype instruction otherwise has no other use and hence is optional for the XML format.

Content Type

The content type can be specified using the 'Content-Type' Header as 'text/html; charset=UTF-8' or can be specified in the first 512 bytes of html using the meta tag as shown below

```
<meta charset="UTF-8">
```

Or in the xml format as

```
<?xml version="1.0" encoding="UTF-8"?>
```

SVG

The html format allows embedding of SVG and MathML inside the HTML 5 document. A very basic SVG example follows.

```
<!doctype html>
.
.
.
.
<body>
<p>
 A green circle:
 <svg> <circle r="50" cx="50" cy="50" fill="green"/> </svg>
</p>
</body>
</html
```

MathML

A basic MathML example follows

```
<!doctype html>
  .
  .
  .
<body>
<p>
<math>
 <mrow>
  <mfrac>
   <mrow>
    <mi>d</mi>
    <mi>y</mi>
   </mrow>
   <mrow>
    <mi>d</mi>
    <mi>x</mi>
   </mrow>
  </mfrac>
  <mo>=</mo>
  <mfrac>
   <mn>1</mn>
   <msup>
    <mi>y</mi>
    <mn>2</mn>
   </msup>
  </mfrac>
 </mrow>
</math>
</p>
</body>
</html>
```

Semantics Examples

```
<body ononline="updatestatus(true)"
    onoffline="updatestatus(false)"
    onload="updatestatus(navigator.onLine)" onerror="reportanerror()">
```

The above example shows the various events available on the body tag. The 'onload' calls our 'updatestatus' event with the current online status using navigator.online. After the document gets loaded and every time it's online status changes the 'online' and 'offline' events get fired calling the updatestatus function. If there is an error on the page the 'error' event gets fired and calls the reportanerror function.

```
<article>
 <hgroup>
 <h1>Apples</h1>
 <h2>Tasty, delicious fruit!</h2>
 </hgroup>
 <p>The apple is the pomaceous fruit of the apple tree.</p>
 <section>
 <h1>Red Delicious</h1>
 <p>These bright red apples are the most common found in many
 supermarkets.</p>
 </section>
 <section>
 <h1>Granny Smith</h1>
 <p>These juicy, green apples make a great filling for
 apple pies.</p>
 </section>
 </article>
```

An hrgoup is meant to contain the heading of an article or a section. It is used instead of the header when there are more than h1...h6 elements that need to be shown.

An article can have many sections. And is intended to be a self contained portion of the web page which is intended to be reusable.

A section is a section of the generic document or application section e.g. a tab on the webpage.

```
<body>
 <header>
 <h1>Wake up sheeple!</h1>
 <nav>
 <h1>Navigation</h1>
 <ul>
 <li><a href="articles.html">Index of all articles</a></li>
 <li><a href="today.html">Things sheeple need to wake up for today</a></li>
 </ul>
 </nav>
 </header>
 <div>
 <article>
```

```
<header>
 <h1>My Day at the Beach</h1>
</header>
<div>
 <p>Today I went to the beach and had a lot of fun.</p>
 ...more content...
</div>
<footer>
 <p>Posted <time pubdate datetime="2009-10-10T14:36-08:00">Thursday</time>.</p>
</footer>
</article>
...more blog posts...
</div>
<footer>
<p>Copyright © 2006 The Example Company</p>
</footer>
</body>
```

Both section and article can have a header and footer. A body is an implicit article and can have its own header and footer. The nav tag is used to denote menus and toolbars used for navigation. It is a section with navigation links.

A header is meant to contain h1..h6 elements, navigational links, logos, icons, table of contents or a search form. A footer is meant to contain links to related documents, information about the author, copyright etc.

```
<p> Monty goes to Switzerland to find his father...</p>

<aside>
 <h1>Switzerland</h1>
 <p>Switzerland, a land-locked country in the middle of geographic
 Europe, has not joined the geopolitical European Union, though it is a signatory to a number of
European treaties.</p>
</aside>

<p> After 2 days of travel he finally landed in Switzerland and checked into the hotel suite his mother
had booked for him...</p>
```

An aside section is meant to contain tangential content in relation to the main article. Typically seen as sidebars, polls, advertisements etc.

```
<article>
...
<address>
 <A href="../People/Raggett/">Dave Raggett</A>,
 <A href="../People/Arnaud/">Arnaud Le Hors</A>,
 contact persons for the <A href="Activity">W3C HTML Activity</A>
```

```
</address>
...
</article>
```

An address tag is meant to contain the contact details applicable to the containing section or article (or body).

```
<figure id="l4">
<figcaption>Listing 4. The primary core interface API declaration.</figcaption>
<pre><code>interface PrimaryCore {
boolean verifyDataLine();
void sendData(in sequence&lt;byte> data);
void initSelfDestruct();
}</code></pre>
</figure>
```

The figure tag is used to contain media, images (i.e figures) or even a presentation text. The figcaption tag is used to add a caption to the figure.

Fallback

Since all of the new HTML5 tags are not widely supported they contain a fallback option which gets rendered on browsers which don't support the specific HTML 5 tag. For example a canvas tag is as follows

```
<canvas id="stockGraph" width="150" height="150">
</canvas>
```

It renders a canvas of 150x150 pixels with the id 'stockGraph'. On browsers which do not support the canvas tag we can do something like

```
<canvas id="stockGraph" width="150" height="150">
 current stock price: $3.15 +0.15
</canvas>
```

Which when executed on a pre HTML 5 browser will render the fallback text 'current stock price: $3.15 +0.15'

WebForms

WebForms are enhancements to presentation of forms on the browser. These are additional input types that the HTML 5 compliant browsers will render for you e.g. Date, Url types etc. In some cases this will involve validation on the browser preventing an erroneous submission and in other cases like Date will render a date chooser which till now was achieved by the use of third party controls and libraries. We will create one small form page to see all these in action. Please create a webforms.html page in notepad with the following contents.

webforms.html code

```html
<!DOCTYPE html>

<html>
<head>
<meta charset="utf-8">
<title>WebForms</title>
</head>
<body>
<section id="wrapper">
  <header>
    <h1>WebForms</h1>
  </header>
<article>
  <form>
    Name <input name="name" placeholder="Enter Your Full Name" autofocus><br />
    Address <input name="address" placeholder="Enter Your Current Address" /><br />
    Email <input name="email" type="email"><br />
    Blog Url <input name="url" type="url"><br />
    Number <input name="number" type="number" min="0" max="100" step="5" value="50"><br />
    Range <input name="range" type="range" min="0" max="100" step="5" value="50"><br />
    Date <input name="date" type="date"><br />
    Month <input name="month" type="month"><br />
    Week <input name="week" type="week"><br />
    Time <input name="time" type="time"><br />
    Datetime <input name="datetime" type="datetime"><br />
    Datetime Local <input name="datetimelocal" type="datetime-local"><br />
    Search Query <input name="query" type="search"><br />
    Color <input name="color" type="color"><br />
    <input type="submit" value="Submit">

  </form>
</article>
</section>
</body>
</html>
```

The 'placeholder' attribute will display the placeholder text in the input control until the time the user enters something upon which it will automatically get removed without the user having to manually delete the placeholder text. 'autofocus' attribute places the focus on the said control which is ready to receive keyboard input.

The 'email' type causes a textbox input value to be validated as an email. Similarly for 'Url' which causes basic Url validation.

The 'number' type renders a number box with up/down arrows to select the number in the steps specified and with the given default value. The 'range' type is like the number type but it renders a slider to select the number. 'date', 'month', 'week', 'time', 'datetime' and 'datetimelocal' are used to enter dates and times with various restrictions. This is rendered with a date picker and a time selector control.

The 'search' type is intended to render a rounded search box with a cross to remove the search query. The 'color' type is supposed to render a color picker which returns a hex string of the color code.

Next, let's see how far these have been implemented in various browsers.

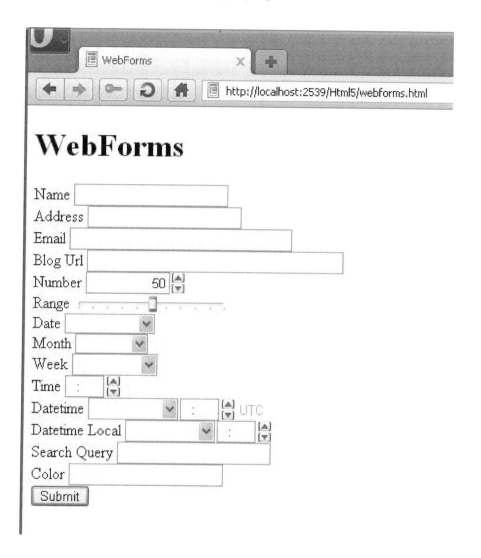

Figure 1 - Opera Rendering the WebForm

Opera seems to have implemented the most of the WebForms support in HTML 5. Except for the 'search' and 'color' types, placeholder and autofocus attributes. Email and Url validations are implemented.

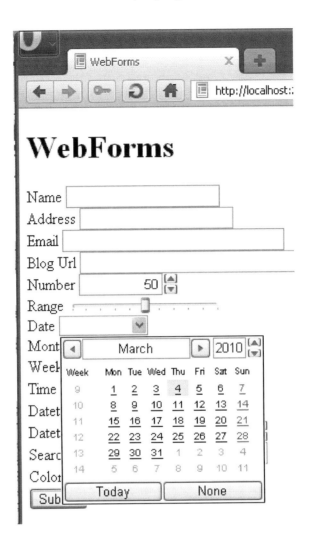

Figure 2 - Opera Rendering the DatePicker

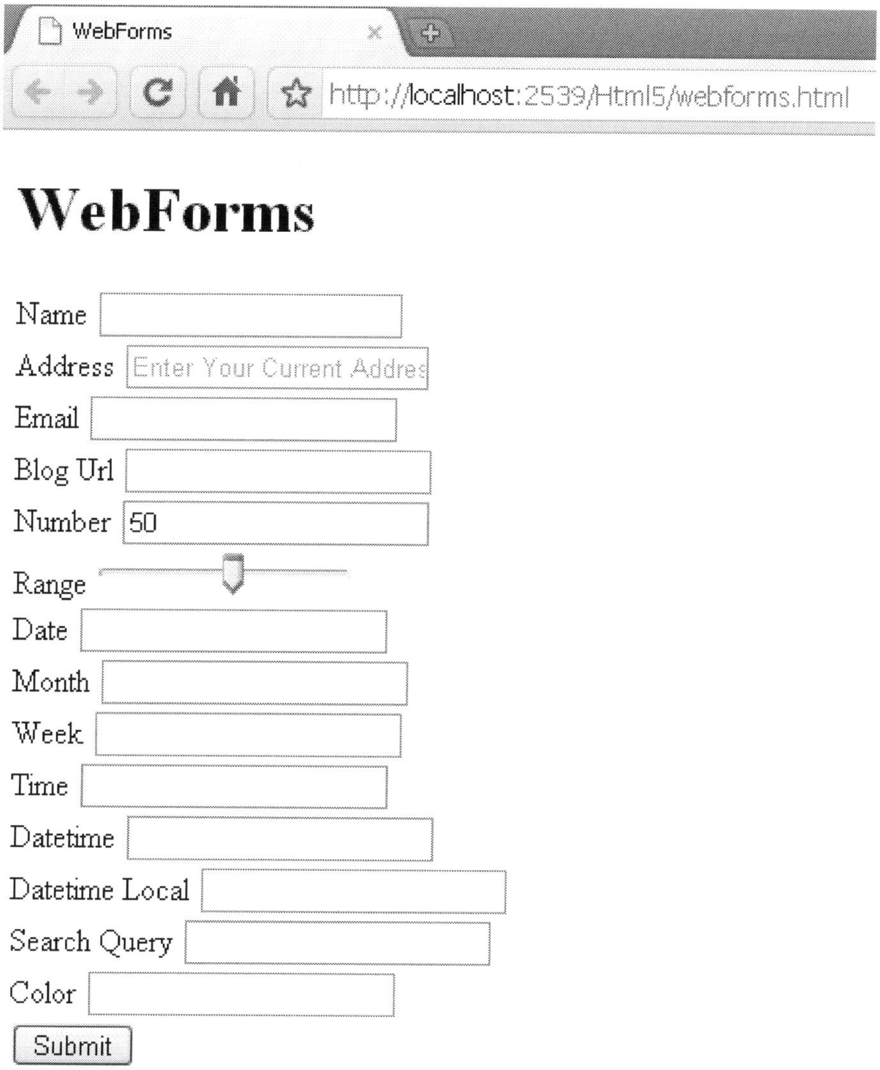

Figure 3 - Chrome Has Not Implemented HTML5 WebForms

Figure 4 - Firefox Has Not Implemented HTML5 WebForms

Figure 5 - IE8 Has Not Implemented HTML5 WebForms

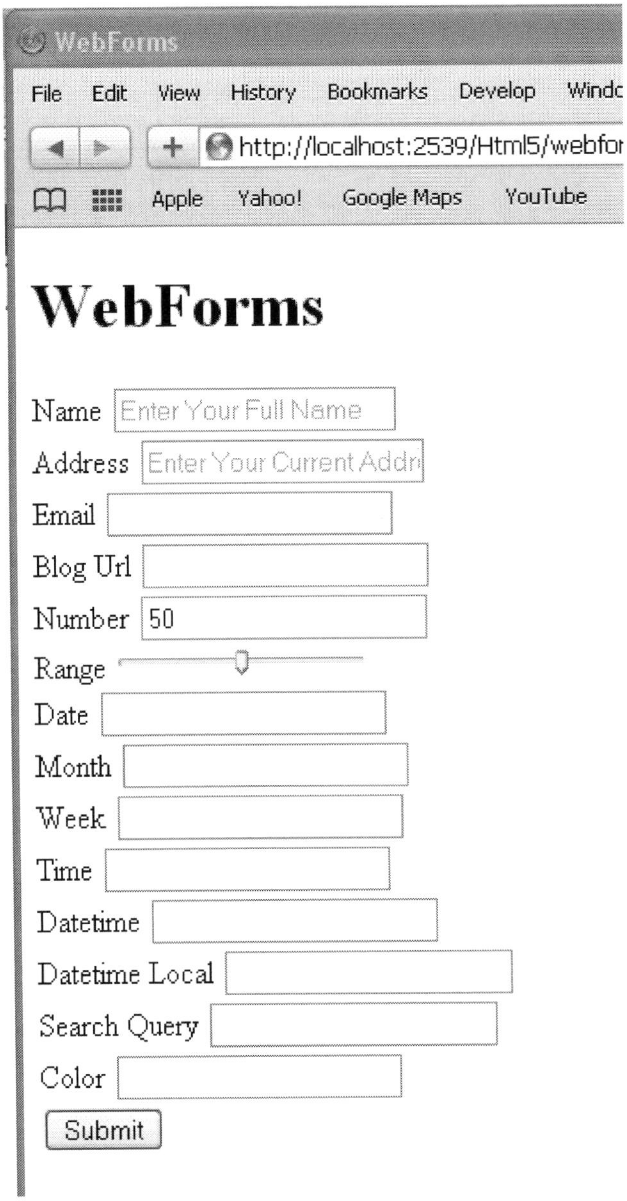

Figure 6 - Safari Has Not Implemented HTML5 WebForms

Chapter 2- Canvas

Let's create a small basic canvas drawing web page 'canvas2d.html' with the following contents.

canvas2d.html Code

```html
<!DOCTYPE html>

<html>
<head>
<meta http-equiv="Content-Type" content="text/html; charset=ISO-8859-1">
<title>Canvas 2D example</title>
<script type="text/javascript" charset="utf-8" src="js/jquery-1.3.2.js"></script>
<script type="text/javascript">
  $(document).ready(function () {
    var canvas = document.getElementById('stockGraph');
    var ctx = canvas.getContext('2d');

    // draw a rectangle
    ctx.fillStyle = "rgba(0, 0, 200, 0.5)";
    ctx.fillRect(30, 30, 55, 50);

    // draw a face

    ctx.beginPath();
    ctx.arc(175, 75, 50, 0, Math.PI * 2, true); // Outer circle
    ctx.moveTo(210, 75);
    ctx.arc(175, 75, 35, 0, Math.PI, false);   // Mouth (clockwise)
    ctx.moveTo(165, 65);
    ctx.arc(160, 65, 5, 0, Math.PI * 2, true);  // Left eye
    ctx.moveTo(195, 65);
    ctx.arc(190, 65, 5, 0, Math.PI * 2, true);  // Right eye
    ctx.stroke();

    // Filled triangle
    ctx.beginPath();
    ctx.moveTo(25, 125);
    ctx.lineTo(105, 125);
    ctx.lineTo(25, 205);
    ctx.fill();

    // Stroked triangle
    ctx.beginPath();
    ctx.moveTo(125, 225);
    ctx.lineTo(125, 145);
    ctx.lineTo(45, 225);
    ctx.closePath();
    ctx.stroke();
```

```
    //arcs & circles
    for (var i = 0; i < 4; i++) {
        for (var j = 0; j < 3; j++) {
            ctx.beginPath();
            var x = 325 + j * 50;          // x coordinate
            var y = 25 + i * 50;           // y coordinate
            var radius = 20;               // Arc radius
            var startAngle = 0;            // Starting point on circle
            var endAngle = Math.PI + (Math.PI * j) / 2; // End point on circle
            var anticlockwise = i % 2 == 0 ? false : true; // clockwise or anticlockwise

            ctx.arc(x, y, radius, startAngle, endAngle, anticlockwise);

            if (i > 1) {
                ctx.fill();
            } else {
                ctx.stroke();
            }
        }
    }

    //bezier curves
    ctx.beginPath();
    ctx.moveTo(275, 225);
    ctx.quadraticCurveTo(225, 225, 225, 262.5);
    ctx.quadraticCurveTo(225, 300, 250, 300);
    ctx.quadraticCurveTo(250, 320, 230, 325);
    ctx.quadraticCurveTo(260, 320, 265, 300);
    ctx.quadraticCurveTo(325, 300, 325, 262.5);
    ctx.quadraticCurveTo(325, 225, 275, 225);
    ctx.stroke();

    ctx.beginPath();
    ctx.moveTo(75, 250);
    ctx.bezierCurveTo(75, 247, 70, 235, 50, 235);
    ctx.bezierCurveTo(20, 235, 20, 272.5, 20, 272.5);
    ctx.bezierCurveTo(20, 290, 40, 312, 75, 330);
    ctx.bezierCurveTo(110, 312, 130, 290, 130, 272.5);
    ctx.bezierCurveTo(130, 272.5, 130, 235, 100, 235);
    ctx.bezierCurveTo(85, 235, 75, 247, 75, 250);
    ctx.fill();


});
</script>
</head>
<body>
    <canvas id="stockGraph" width="640" height="480">
    </canvas>

</body>
</html>
```

```
<canvas id="stockGraph" width="640" height="480">
 </canvas>
```

The canvas tag hosts the canvas on which we will draw the shapes. The Javascript code executes and draws shapes on the canvas when the Document Ready event fires.

Let's quickly try it out in various browsers.

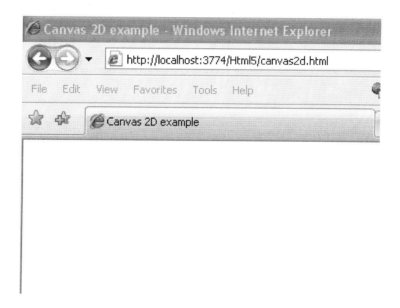

Figure 7 - Shapes & Canvas Don't Work in IE

Figure 8 - Shapes Working in Chrome

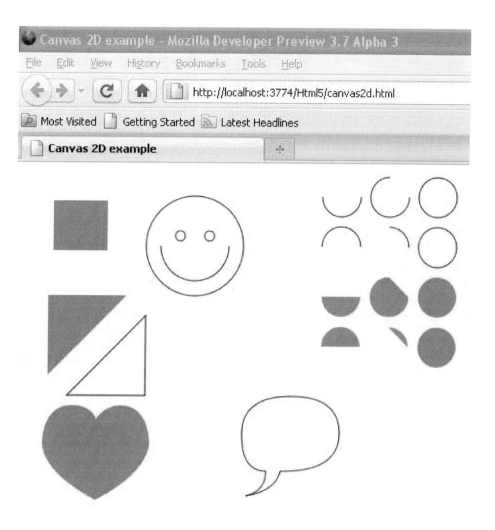

Figure 9 - Shapes Working in Firefox

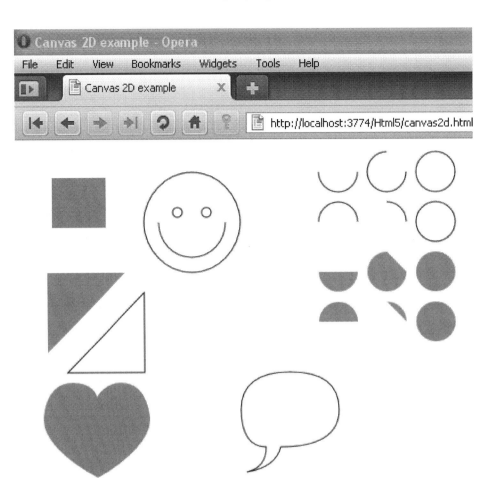

Figure 10 - Shapes Working in Opera

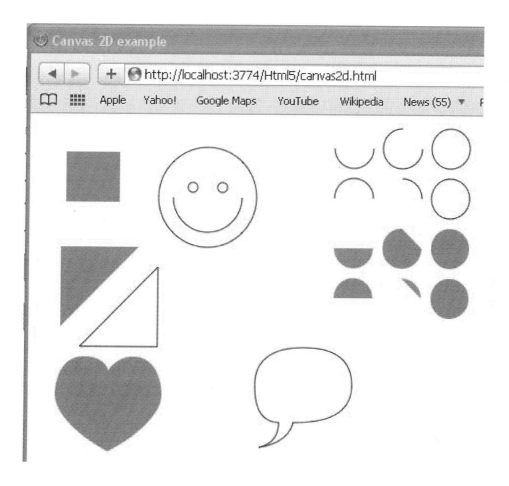

Figure 11 - Shapes Working in Safari

A Quick Walkthrough of the Specifications

A basic canvas tag is as follows

```
<canvas id="stockGraph" width="150" height="150">
</canvas>
```

The canvas tag just has two attributes width & height which can also be set using CSS along with CSS styling.

In javascript we can get a reference to the context as follows.

```
var canvas = document.getElementById('stockGraph');
var ctx = canvas.getContext('2d');
```

The above code gets a reference to the Canvas tag and then a reference to its 2d context.

```
ctx.fillStyle = "rgba(0, 0, 200, 0.5)";  // or ctx.fillStyle = "rgb(0,0,200)";
ctx.fillRect (30, 30, 55, 50);
```

The above code sets a fillStyle with the 'rgba' value which stands for Red Blue Green and Alpha Transparency value. It then draws a filled rectangle.

Unlike SVG canvas supports only one primitive shape Rectangle all other shapes have to be drawn using Paths. The rectangle related functions are as follows

- fillRect(x,y,width,height) : Draws a filled rectangle
- strokeRect(x,y,width,height) : Draws a rectangular outline
- clearRect(x,y,width,height) : Clears the specified area and makes it fully transparent

To make shapes using Paths we need the following

- beginPath()
- closePath()
- stroke()
- fill()

For example

```
ctx.beginPath();
ctx.arc(75,75,50,0,Math.PI*2,true); // Outer circle
ctx.moveTo(110,75);
ctx.arc(75,75,35,0,Math.PI,false);   // Mouth (clockwise)
ctx.moveTo(65,65);
ctx.arc(60,65,5,0,Math.PI*2,true);  // Left eye
ctx.moveTo(95,65);
ctx.arc(90,65,5,0,Math.PI*2,true);  // Right eye
ctx.stroke();
```

For drawing a line we use the lineTo method

lineTo(x, y)

For example

```
// Filled triangle
ctx.beginPath();
ctx.moveTo(25,25);
ctx.lineTo(105,25);
ctx.lineTo(25,105);
ctx.fill();


// Stroked triangle
ctx.beginPath();
ctx.moveTo(125,125);
ctx.lineTo(125,45);
ctx.lineTo(45,125);
ctx.closePath();
ctx.stroke();
```

To make an Arc or Circles we use the 'arc' method

arc(x, y, radius, startAngle, endAngle, anticlockwise)

For example

```
for(var i=0;i<4;i++){
  for(var j=0;j<3;j++){
    ctx.beginPath();
    var x            = 25+j*50;          // x coordinate
    var y            = 25+i*50;          // y coordinate
    var radius       = 20;              // Arc radius
    var startAngle   = 0;                  // Starting point on circle
    var endAngle     = Math.PI+(Math.PI*j)/2; // End point on circle
    var anticlockwise = i%2==0 ? false : true; // clockwise or anticlockwise
```

```
  ctx.arc(x,y,radius,startAngle,endAngle, anticlockwise);

 if (i>1){
   ctx.fill();
 } else {
   ctx.stroke();
 }
 }
}
```

To draw a Bezier curve we use the following

```
quadraticCurveTo(cp1x, cp1y, x, y)
bezierCurveTo(cp1x, cp1y, cp2x, cp2y, x, y)
```

quadraticCurve has one control point and is a quadratic Bezier curve while the bezierCurveTo has two control points and draws a cubic bezier curve.

For example

```
ctx.beginPath();
ctx.moveTo(275,225);
ctx.quadraticCurveTo(225,225,25,62.5);
ctx.quadraticCurveTo(225,300,50,100);
ctx.quadraticCurveTo(250,320,30,125);
ctx.quadraticCurveTo(260,320,65,100);
ctx.quadraticCurveTo(325,300,125,62.5);
ctx.quadraticCurveTo(325,225,75,25);
ctx.stroke();

ctx.beginPath();
ctx.moveTo(75,40);
ctx.bezierCurveTo(75,37,70,25,50,25);
ctx.bezierCurveTo(20,25,20,62.5,20,62.5);
ctx.bezierCurveTo(20,80,40,102,75,120);
ctx.bezierCurveTo(110,102,130,80,130,62.5);
ctx.bezierCurveTo(130,62.5,130,25,100,25);
```

```
ctx.bezierCurveTo(85,25,75,37,75,40);
ctx.fill();
```

Besides the above we can draw rectangular shapes directly to the path using

```
rect(x, y, width, height)
```

Retrospective

We have covered basic drawing on the canvas. We have left Images, Transitions and Compositing to the reader to try on his own.

Chapter 3- Drag & Drop

While Drag Drop functionality was implemented earlier using various javascript libraries available for development. In this chapter we are going to see how to implement Native Drag Drop capabilities which are a part of HTML 5.

Let's start rightaway by creating a small Drag Drop page dragdrop.html in notepad with the following contents.

dragdrop.html code

```
<!DOCTYPE html>

<html>
<head>
<meta http-equiv="Content-Type" content="text/html; charset=ISO-8859-1">
<title>Native Drag Drop</title>
<script type="text/javascript" charset="utf-8" src="js/jquery-1.3.2.js"></script>
<script type="text/javascript">
    $(document).ready(function() {
        $('.canbedragged').each(function(){
            $(this).attr('draggable', 'true')
            .bind('dragstart', function(ev) {
                ev.originalEvent.dataTransfer.effectAllowed = 'move';
                var dt = ev.originalEvent.dataTransfer;
                dt.setData("Color", $(this).text());
                return true;
            })
            .bind('dragend', function(ev) {
                return false;
            });
        });
        $('.canbedroppedinto').each(function(){
            $(this).bind('dragenter', function(ev) {
                $(ev.target).addClass('dragover');
                return false;
            })
            .bind('dragleave', function(ev) {
                $(ev.target).removeClass('dragover');
                return false;
            })
            .bind('dragover', function(ev) {
                return false;
            })
            .bind('drop', function(ev) {
                var dt = ev.originalEvent.dataTransfer;
                this.innerHTML += '<div class="canbedragged" style="border:dotted
```

```
red;background: white">'+dt.getData('Color')+'</div>'
                return false;
            });
        });
    });

</script>
</head>
<body>

<table border="1" bgcolor="grey">
        <tr>
                <td>
                        <div style="width:250px; height:400px;">
                                <b>Pallete</b>
                                <div class="canbedragged" style="border:dotted red;background:
white">Yellow</div>
                                <div class="canbedragged" style="border:dotted red;background:
white">Blue</div>
                                <div class="canbedragged" style="border:dotted red;background:
white">Green</div>
                        </div>
                </td>
                <td>
                        <div class="canbedroppedinto" style="width:250px; height:400px;">
                                <b>Canvas</b>
                        </div>
                </td>
        </tr>
</table>
</body>
</html>
```

Let's understand what we are doing in the above piece of code.

```
<table border="1" bgcolor="grey">
```

Renders a table with 1 pixel border and grey background color. It has one Row (tr) and has two columns (td). The first table column (left one) is implemented as follows

```
<div style="width:250px; height:400px;">
                                <b>Pallete</b>
                                <div class="canbedragged" style="border:dotted red;background:
white">Yellow</div>
```

```
                              <div class="canbedragged" style="border:dotted red;background:
white">Blue</div>
                              <div class="canbedragged" style="border:dotted red;background:
white">Green</div>
                    </div>
```

This is basically one div containing 3 child divs. The parent div is of 400x250 pixel size and contains the bold text 'Pallete' below which there are 3 child divs with dotted red border and white background color containing the texts Yellow, Blue and Green respectively. The child divs have a class 'canbedragged' which will be used by our javascript to make them draggable. The second table column is implemented as follows.

```
<div class="canbedroppedinto" style="width:250px; height:400px;">
        <b>Canvas</b>
</div>
```

It is of size 400x250 pixels and has a bold text 'Canvas' and has the style 'canbedroppedinto'. Our javascript will use the class name to bind the droppable functionality to it. Let's look at the javascrip functionality.

```
<script type="text/javascript" charset="utf-8" src="js/jquery-1.3.2.js"></script>
```

This line includes the JQuery javascript file into the html page. We will be using JQuery for implementing drag and drop.

```
$(document).ready(function() {
...

});
```

The document ready function is used to run our code after the html page finishes loading.

We run two pieces of code the first one is

```
$('.canbedragged').each(function(){
        $(this).attr('draggable', 'true')
        .bind('dragstart', function(ev) {
            ev.originalEvent.dataTransfer.effectAllowed = 'move';
            var dt = ev.originalEvent.dataTransfer;
            dt.setData("Color", $(this).text());
            return true;
        })
        .bind('dragend', function(ev) {
            return false;
        });
    });
```

In this code we select all divs which have the style canbedragged
(.canbedragged selector) and for each of them we set the 'draggable' attribute to
true and then we bind the dragstart event to our function. Which allows the move
effect (we shall see it in effect when we run the page and drag drop items, in a
bit). We get the innerText of the dragged div using $(this).text() which will be
either Yellow/Blue/Green and set it in the DataTransfer object which can be
recovered by the drop target when the drop is made in effect transferring the
object/data with the drag drop. There is another chained bind statement which
gets called after the drag has ended whether it was cancelled or completed
eitherway. We return false to prevent further chain of events handlers (default
handler or other handlers) from firing.

The second piece of code is for the drop target div, the one with the
'canbedroppedinto' style.

```
$('.canbedroppedinto').each(function(){
        $(this).bind('dragenter', function(ev) {
            $(ev.target).addClass('dragover');
            return false;
        })
        .bind('dragleave', function(ev) {
            $(ev.target).removeClass('dragover');
            return false;
        })
        .bind('dragover', function(ev) {
            return false;
        })
```

```
                .bind('drop', function(ev) {
                    var dt = ev.originalEvent.dataTransfer;
                    this.innerHTML += '<div class="canbedragged" style="border:dotted
red;background: white">'+dt.getData('Color')+'</div>'
                    return false;
                });
            });
    });
```

We bind to a couple of events. On dragenter we add the class dragover to the target div. On dragleave we remove the class dragover from the target div. On drop we recover the data transfer object and recover the color passed and we append an html snippet to the innerHTML of the target div in effect drawing the dropped object. In every case of binding we return false and prevent further event handlers from firing.

Let's try out a drag drop in Firefox. While dragging we can see the move effect…shown below…

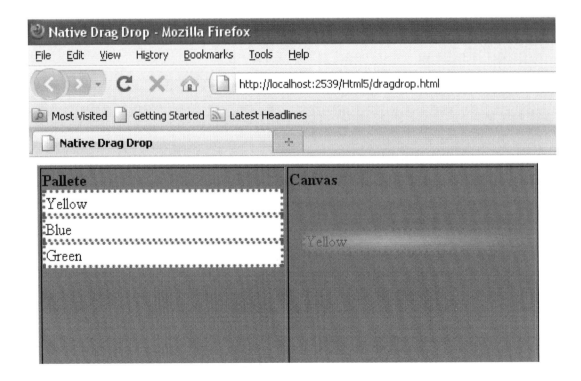

Figure 12 - Move Effect While Dragging

After we drag Yellow and Green the page looks like...

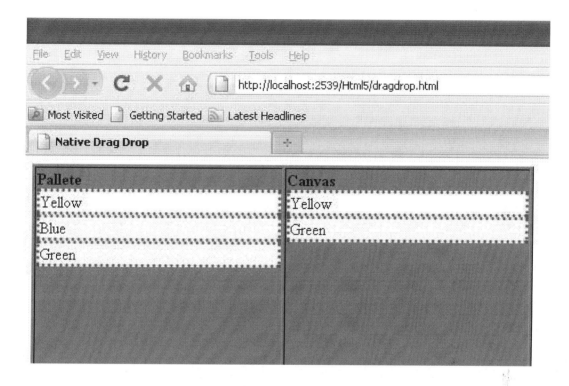

Figure 13 - Yellow & Green Dropped

Let's see if this works in other browsers.

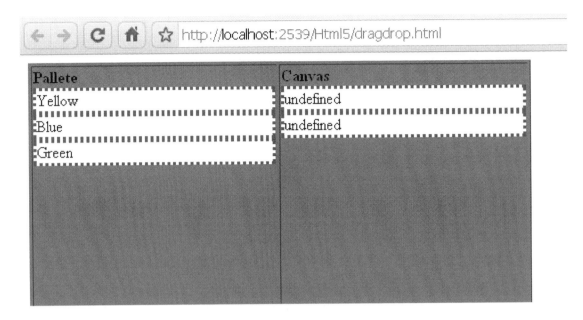

Figure 14 - Drag Drop in Chrome

There is some silent data transfer error in Chrome. We will need to do some javascript wizardry to make this work.

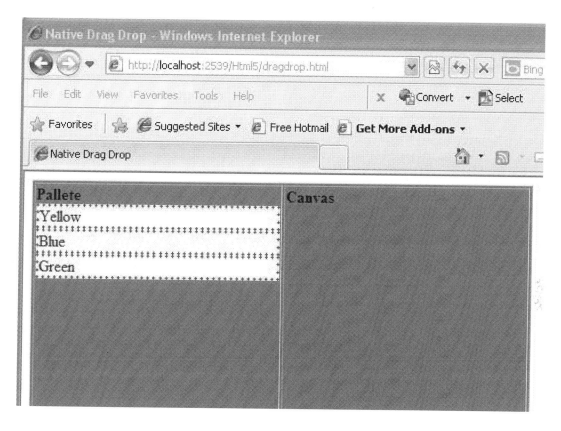

Figure 15 - Drag Drop doesn't work in IE 8

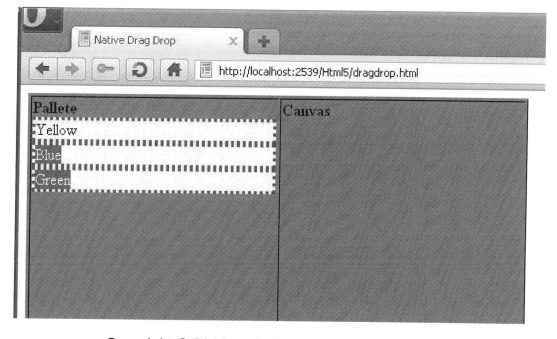

Figure 16 - Drag Drop doesn't work in Opera

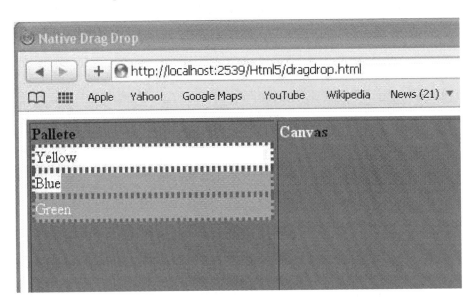

Figure 17 - Drag Drop doesn't work in Safari

A Quick Walkthrough of the Specifications

The native drag drop support works by marking any html tag with the draggable attribute, setting it to true for that element.

Various events will be fired during drag and drop which are as follows

- dragstart – a drag has been started with the dragged element as the event target

- drag – the mouse has moved with the drag event as the event target

- dragenter – the dragged element has moved into a droppable target with the latter as the event target

- dragover – the dragged element has moved over a droppable target with the latter as the event target

- dragleave – the dragged element has moved out of the droppable target, with the latter as the event target

- drop – the dragged element has been successfully dropped on the droppable target with the latter as the event target.

- dragend - the drag has ended either successfully or unsuccessfully

The event provides a property called dataTransfer as 'event.originalEvent.dataTransfer' which can be used for the transmission of user defined data.

The dataTransfer can be used to specify drop effects as follows

- none - no operation is permitted

- copy - copy only

- move - move only

- link - link only

- copyMove - copy or move only

- copyLink - copy or link only

- linkMove - link or move only

- all - copy, move, or link

The dragover event handler can check the drop effect and return 'true' to cancel the drag or 'false' to allow it. The drop effect has to make sense in the logical context of the application.

Retrospective

We created a smiple native drag drop application and tried it out in various browsers. We also went through the specifications for the drag drop feature. Drag drop doesn't work in Safar or Opera and in Chrome there is some issue with data transfer.

Chapter 4- History

HTML 5 allows browser history manipulations along with passing of state from one page to another. Let's try out this with an example. Create history.html in a notepad with the following contents.

history.html code

```html
<!DOCTYPE html>
<!-- This feature was tested in Firefox 3.7 alpha from http://www.brothersoft.com/firefox-download-59843.html -->
<html>
<head>
<meta http-equiv="Content-Type" content="text/html; charset=ISO-8859-1">
<title>History</title>
<script type="text/javascript" charset="utf-8" src="js/jquery-1.3.2.js"></script>

<script type="text/javascript">
  function go() {
    var historyindex = $('#historyindex').val();
    window.history.go(historyindex);
  }

  function back() {
    window.history.back();
  }

  function forward() {
    window.history.forward();
  }

  function pushstate() {
    var statepayload = $('#statepayload').val();
    var stateObj = { payload: statepayload };
    history.pushState(stateObj, "insertedpage", "history.html");
    //history.replaceState(stateObj, "insertedpage", "history.html");
  }

  $(document).ready(new function () {
    var historylength = window.history.length;
    $('#historylength').html("<h2>" + historylength + "</h2>");
  });

  window.onpopstate = function (event) {
    var historystate = "location: " + document.location + ", state: " + event.state.payload;
    $('#historystate').html("<h2>" + historystate + "</h2>");
  };

</script>
```

```
</head>
<body>
  <h1>History</h1>
  <div id="historylength"></div><br />
  <div id="historystate"></div><br/>
  History <input id="historyindex" type="text" value="-1"/><input type="button" value="Go!"
onclick="go();"/><br />
  <input type="button" value="Back!" onclick="back();" /><input type="button" value="Forward!"
onclick="forward();" /><br />
  <h2>Push State</h2>
  State Payload <input id="statepayload" type="text" /><input type="button" value="Push State"
onclick="pushstate();"/><br />

</body>
</html>
```

```
function go() {
    var historyindex = $('#historyindex').val();
    window.history.go(historyindex);
}
```

The go function navigates to the history item with the given history index. We use the value provided in the historyindex text box for the navigation.

```
function back() {
    window.history.back();
}

function forward() {
    window.history.forward();
}
```

The back and forward functions navigate the browser back and forward one position in history respectively.

```
function pushstate() {
    var statepayload = $('#statepayload').val();
    var stateObj = { payload: statepayload };
    history.pushState(stateObj, "insertedpage", "history.html");
    //history.replaceState(stateObj, "insertedpage", "history.html");
}
```

The pushstate function takes a value input by the user from the statepayload textbox and sets it as the value of payload attribute in a json object. It then pushes the state object with history.html as the page url. This is the same url as that of the current page incidently as we haven't created multiple pages for the demo.

```
$(document).ready(new function () {
    var historylength = window.history.length;
    $('#historylength').html("<h2>" + historylength + "</h2>");
});
```

The above piece of code executes when the document is ready and retrieves the length of the history and sets it as the content of the historylength div.

```
window.onpopstate = function (event) {
    var historystate = "location: " + document.location + ", state: " + event.state.payload;
    $('#historystate').html("<h2>" + historystate + "</h2>");
};
```

The above event handler hooks onto 'onpopstate' event and sets the document location and the payload into the contents of the historystate div.

```
<div id="historylength"></div><br />
<div id="historystate"></div><br/>
```

These are the divs which display the history length and the history state.

```
History <input id="historyindex" type="text" value="-1"/><input type="button" value="Go!"
onclick="go();"/><br />
    <input type="button" value="Back!" onclick="back();" /><input type="button" value="Forward!"
onclick="forward();" /><br />
```

The above code renders the historyindex textbox with -1 prefilled. It renders the Go! Button which can be used to navigate to a history item with the given history index.

It also renders the Back! And Forward! Buttons which allow us to go back and forward one history item at a time.

State Payload <input id="statepayload" type="text" /><input type="button" value="Push State" onclick="pushstate();"/>

The above code renders the statepayload textbox which lets the user enter the text to be set as payload. It also renders the Push State button which pushes the state.

Let's take it for a spin. The only browser which seems to support the history state pushing functionality seems to be Firefox 3.7 Alpha. Lets open it up and enter 'http://google.com' and then after it finishes loading enter the url for this page.

Enter 'This-is-the-state-I-set' in the state textbox and push state. Now enter 'http://yahoo.com' and after it finishes loading press the back button on the browser. The state event will get fired and the state will get displayed on the page. See below.

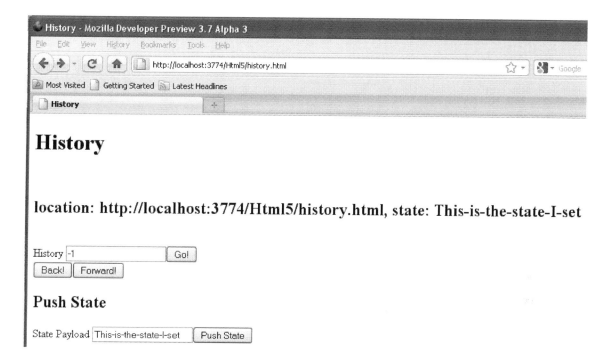

Figure 18 - 'onpopstate' Event Recovering State in Firefox

The Go!, Back! And Forward! Features are functional in Firefox. But the history length is not being shown. Let's try the features in the other browsers.

History

Push State

Figure 19 - History Features in Opera

The Go!, Back! And Forward! Features work in Opera. History Length and State functionality doesn't work.

Figure 20 - History Features in Safari

The Go!, Back! And Forward! Features work in Safari. History Length and State functionality doesn't work.

Figure 21 - History Features in IE

The Go!, Back! And Forward! Features work in IE. History Length and State functionality doesn't work.

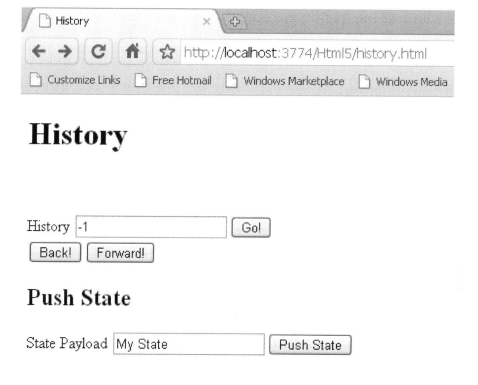

Figure 22 - History Features in Chrome

The Go!, Back! And Forward! Features work in Chrome. History Length and State functionality doesn't work.

A Quick Walkthrough of the Specifications

A sequence of documents in the browsing context is called its session history. URLs with state objects are added to the session history as user/script navigates from page to page.

A state object represents the user interface state. State objects can be added for a page between its entry and the next("forward") entry. When the user navigates back to the page the state object is provided to the page with an event. The history interface is outlined below

- window.history.length - Returns the number of entries in the joint session history.

- window.history.go([delta]) - Goes back or forward the specified number of steps in the joint session history. A zero delta will reload the current page. If the delta is out of range, does nothing.

- window.history.back() - Goes back one step in the joint session history. If there is no previous page, does nothing.

- window.history.forward() - Goes forward one step in the joint session history. If there is no next page, does nothing.

- window.history.pushState(data, title [, url]) - Pushes the given data onto the session history, with the given title, and, if provided, the given URL.

- window.history.replaceState(data, title [, url]) - Updates the current entry in the session history to have the given data, title, and, if provided, URL.

Retrospective

We created a simple web page to test the various history features and tried the page out in various browsers. Firefox seems to support the specification the best, but history.length didn't work in firefox. IR, Chrome, Safari and Opera don't support the state object history feature(s).

Chapter 5- Inline Editing

HTML 5 contains two features for inline editing 'designmode' and 'contenteditable'. Designmode applies to the whole html document usually loaded in an iframe with editing controls on the parent page. While 'contenteditable' is usually set on a div and its contents can be edited. What we build around it is upto us.

Let's try the first example of contenteditable by creating a page 'contenteditable.html' with the following contents.

contenteditable.html Code

```html
<!DOCTYPE html>

<html>
<head>
<meta http-equiv="Content-Type" content="text/html; charset=ISO-8859-1">
<title>Content Editable</title>
<script type="text/javascript" charset="utf-8" src="js/jquery-1.3.2.js"></script>
<script type="text/javascript">

    function doShowHTML() {
        var bodysource = document.getElementById("content").innerHTML;
        bodysource.replace(/</g,'&lt;');
        bodysource.replace(/>/g, '&gt;');
        $('#source').text(bodysource);
    }

    function doInsertLink() {
        var url = prompt("URL:", "http://");
        if (url)
            document.execCommand("createlink", false, url);
    }

    function doInsertTable() {
        var size = prompt("Enter desired rows and columns: (rows|cols)", "2|2");
        if (size) {
            var rowcol = size.split("|");
            if (rowcol.length == 2 && rowcol[0] > 0 && rowcol[0] < 10&& rowcol[1] > 0 && rowcol[1] < 10)
{
                var html = "<table border='1'>";
                for (var row=0; row<rowcol[0]; row++) {
                    html += "<tr>";
                    for (var col=0; col<rowcol[1]; col++) {
```

```
                    html += "<td width='20'></td>";
                }
                html += "</tr>";
            }
            html += "</table>";
            document.execCommand('inserthtml', false, html);
        }
    }
}
</script>
</head>
<body>
  <div id="toolbar">
    <input type="button" id="bold" value="Bold" onclick="document.execCommand('bold', false,
null);"/>
    <input type="button" id="italic" value="Italic" onclick="document.execCommand('italic', false,
null);" />
    <input type="button" id="underline" value="Underline"
onclick="document.execCommand('underline', false, null);"/>
    <input type="button" id="link" value="Link" onclick="doInsertLink();"/>
    <input type="button" id="table" value="Table" onclick="doInsertTable();"/>
    <input type="button" id="showhtml" value="View Source" onclick="doShowHTML();"/>
  </div>
  <br />
  <div id="content" style='border:solid blue;background: white;height: 400px;width: 400px'
contenteditable="true"></div>
  <div id="source" style='border:solid green;background: white;height: 400px;width: 400px' ></div>

</body>
</html>
```

```
<div id="toolbar">
    <input type="button" id="bold" value="Bold" onclick="document.execCommand('bold', false, null);"/>
    <input type="button" id="italic" value="Italic" onclick="document.execCommand('italic', false, null);" />
    <input type="button" id="underline" value="Underline" onclick="document.execCommand('underline',
false, null);"/>
    <input type="button" id="link" value="Link" onclick="doInsertLink();"/>
    <input type="button" id="table" value="Table" onclick="doInsertTable();"/>
    <input type="button" id="showhtml" value="View Source" onclick="doShowHTML();"/>
</div>
```

This div renders the toolbar. The toolbar contains buttons to toggle bold, italic, underline of the current selection and to insert a link or a table, and to show the html source of the editable div. Showhtml button calls the doShowHTML function on being clicked. Table button calls the 'doInsertTable' on being clicked. The Link button calls the 'doInsertLink' on being clicked. While the bold, italic, and underline buttons call the 'document.execCommand()' function on being clicked. They pass the action to the function which is 'bold', 'italic' and 'underline' respectively. The function is a built in browser function which then executes the action on the selected text, anywhere in the document, if it is applicable, usually it is if inside an editable div.

```
<div id="content" style='border:solid blue;background: white;height: 400px;width: 400px'
contenteditable="true"></div>
```

This div hosts the editable content note the attribute contenteditable='true' set on it.

```
<div id="source" style='border:solid green;background: white;height: 400px;width: 400px' ></div>
```

This div will be used to display the html source code of the editable div contents.

```
function doShowHTML() {
    var bodysource = document.getElementById("content").innerHTML;
    bodysource.replace(/</g,'&lt;');
    bodysource.replace(/>/g, '&gt;');
    $('#source').text(bodysource);
}
```

The doShowHTML function gets the html contents of the editable div with the id 'content'. It does a global replacement of '<' and '>' characters with '<' and '>' so that they don't get deleted when being shown as text in the 'source' div. It then sets the html snippet as text in the div with the id 'source'

```
function doInsertLink() {
    var url = prompt("URL:", "http://");
    if (url)
        document.execCommand("createlink", false, url);
}
```

The above function prompts the user for a URL and then calls the
document.execCommand passing 'createlink' action and the user entered URL
as the parameter. This will be applied to the current selection.

```
function doInsertTable() {
    var size = prompt("Enter desired rows and columns: (rows|cols)", "2|2");
    if (size) {
      var rowcol = size.split("|");
      if (rowcol.length == 2 && rowcol[0] > 0 && rowcol[0] < 10&& rowcol[1] > 0 && rowcol[1] < 10) {
        var html = "<table border='1'>";
        for (var row=0; row<rowcol[0]; row++) {
          html += "<tr>";
          for (var col=0; col<rowcol[1]; col++) {
            html += "<td width='20'></td>";
          }
          html += "</tr>";
        }
        html += "</table>";
        document.execCommand('inserthtml', false, html);
      }
    }
}
```

The above function prompts the user to enter the number of rows and columns in
the table. It generates a string snippet of the html of the table to be inserted. And
then calls the document.execCommand passing 'inserthtml' as action and the
string html snippet as the parameter.

We are all set. Let's take this for a spin in the various browsers. We will be
entering 'Hello World' in the editable div and making the word World bold. And
we will click the View Source button.

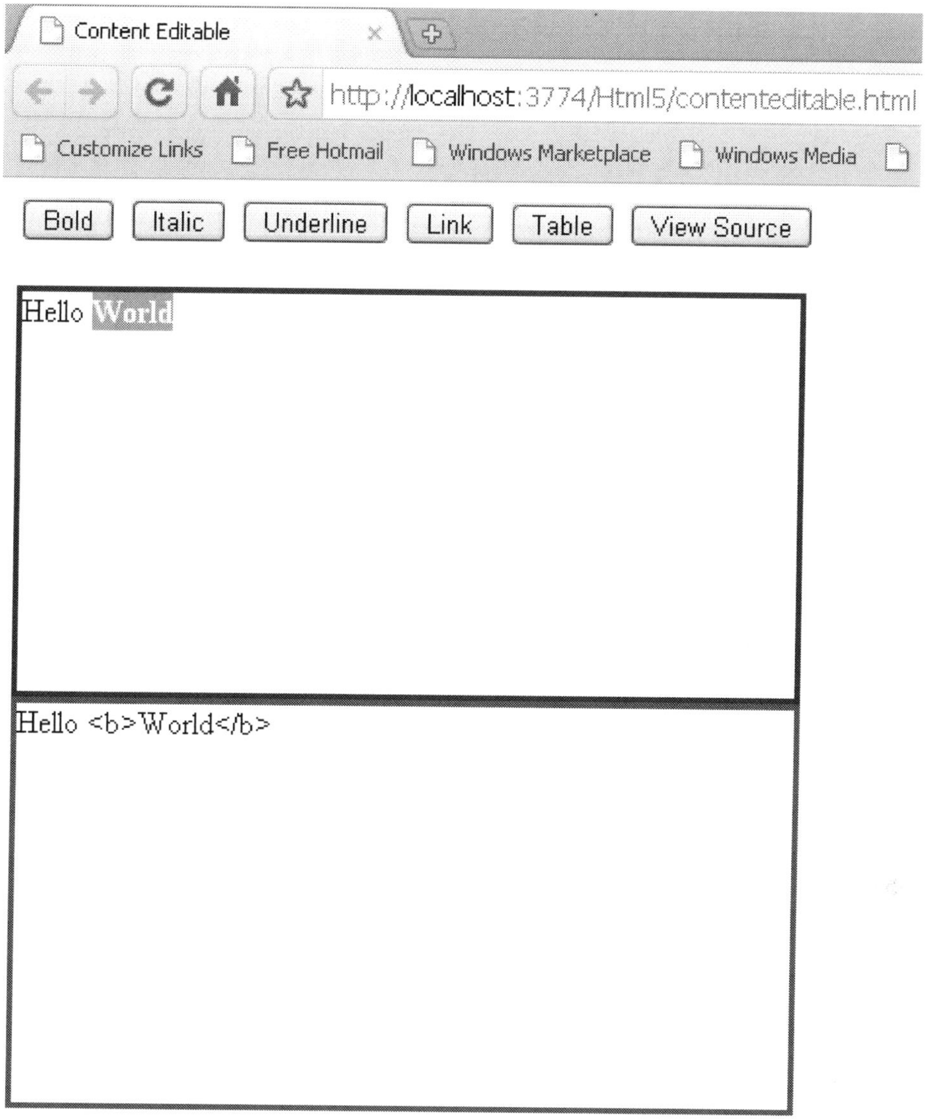

Figure 23 - ContentEditable Working in Chrome

Deploying HTML5

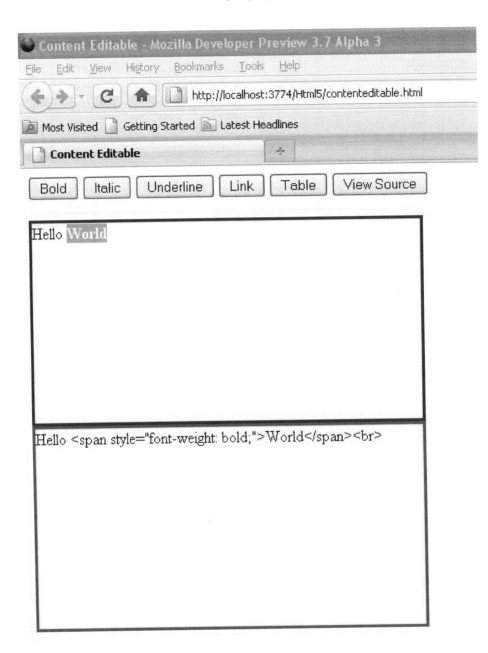

Figure 24 - ContentEditable Working in Firefox

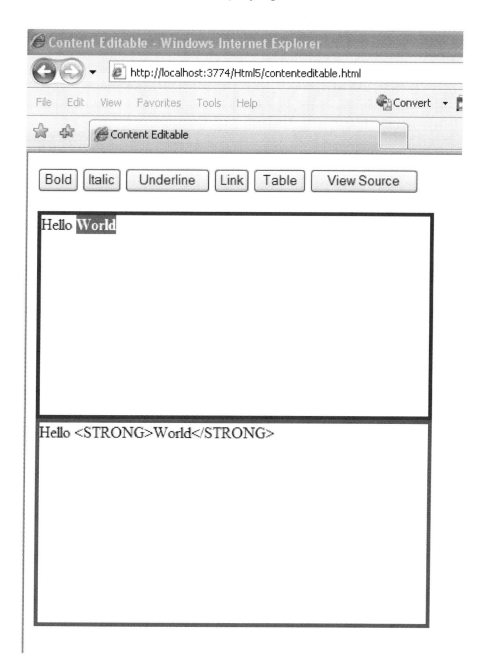

Figure 25 - ContentEditable Working in IE

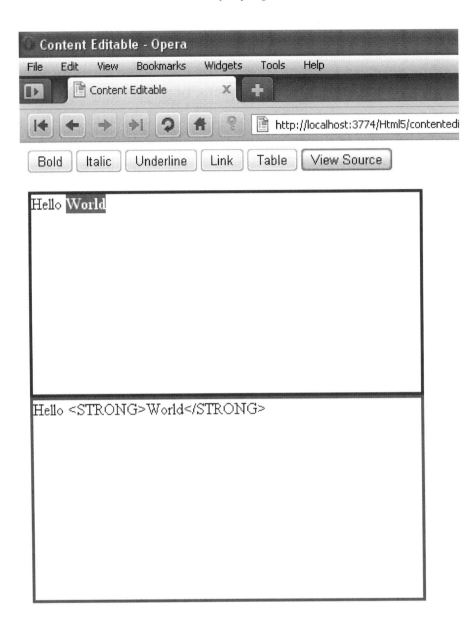

Figure 26 - ContentEditable Working in Opera

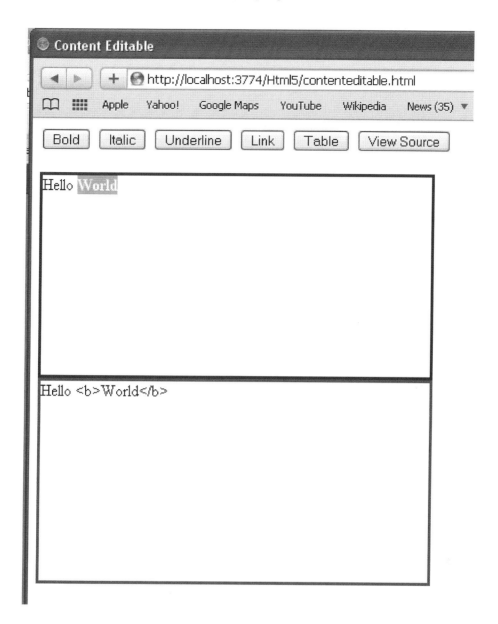

Figure 27 - ContentEditable Working in Safari

Note the generated HTML source for the editable content in each of the browsers. It is very browser specific.

Let's try the 'DesignMode' feature by creating a file 'designmode.html' with the following contents.

designmode.html Code

```html
<!DOCTYPE html>

<html>
<head>
<meta http-equiv="Content-Type" content="text/html; charset=ISO-8859-1">
<title>Design Mode</title>
<script type="text/javascript" charset="utf-8" src="js/jquery-1.3.2.js"></script>
<script type="text/javascript">
  var editor;

  function onload() {
    editor = document.getElementById("content-iframe");
    editor.contentDocument.designMode = "on";
  }

  function doShowHTML() {
    var bodysource = editor.contentDocument.body.innerHTML;
    bodysource.replace(/</g, '&lt;');
    bodysource.replace(/>/g, '&gt;');
    $('#source').text(bodysource);
  }

  function doInsertLink() {
    var url = prompt("URL:", "http://");
    if (url)
      editor.contentDocument.execCommand("createlink", false, url);
  }

  function doInsertTable() {
    var size = prompt("Enter desired rows and columns: (rows|cols)", "2|2");
    if (size) {
      var rowcol = size.split("|");
      if (rowcol.length == 2 && rowcol[0] > 0 && rowcol[0] < 10 && rowcol[1] > 0 && rowcol[1] < 10)
{
          var html = "<table border='1'>";
          for (var row = 0; row < rowcol[0]; row++) {
            html += "<tr>";
            for (var col = 0; col < rowcol[1]; col++) {
              html += "<td width='20'></td>";
            }
            html += "</tr>";
          }
          html += "</table>";
          editor.contentDocument.execCommand('inserthtml', false, html);
      }
    }
  }

  window.addEventListener("load", onload, false);
</script>
</head>
<body>
```

```
  <div id="toolbar">
    <input type="button" id="bold" value="Bold"
onclick="editor.contentDocument.execCommand('bold', false, null);"/>
    <input type="button" id="italic" value="Italic"
onclick="editor.contentDocument.execCommand('italic', false, null);" />
    <input type="button" id="underline" value="Underline"
onclick="editor.contentDocument.execCommand('underline', false, null);"/>
    <input type="button" id="link" value="Link" onclick="doInsertLink();"/>
    <input type="button" id="table" value="Table" onclick="doInsertTable();"/>
    <input type="button" id="showhtml" value="View Source" onclick="doShowHTML();"/>
  </div>
  <br />
  <iframe id="content-iframe" style='border:solid blue;background: white;height: 200px;width: 400px'
src="about:blank"></iframe>
  <div id="source" style='border:solid green;background: white;height: 200px;width: 400px' ></div>

</body>
</html>
```

```
  <div id="toolbar">
    <input type="button" id="bold" value="Bold" onclick="editor.contentDocument.execCommand('bold',
false, null);"/>
    <input type="button" id="italic" value="Italic" onclick="editor.contentDocument.execCommand('italic',
false, null);" />
    <input type="button" id="underline" value="Underline"
onclick="editor.contentDocument.execCommand('underline', false, null);"/>
    <input type="button" id="link" value="Link" onclick="doInsertLink();"/>
    <input type="button" id="table" value="Table" onclick="doInsertTable();"/>
    <input type="button" id="showhtml" value="View Source" onclick="doShowHTML();"/>
  </div>
```

This div renders the toolbar. The toolbar contains buttons to toggle bold, italic, underline of the current selection and to insert a link or a table, and to show the html source of the editable div. Showhtml button calls the doShowHTML function on being clicked. Table button calls the 'doInsertTable' on being clicked. The Link button calls the 'doInsertLink' on being clicked. While the bold, italic, and underline buttons call the 'contentDocument.execCommand()' function on the iframe on being clicked. They pass the action to the function which is 'bold', 'italic' and 'underline' respectively. The function is a built in browser function which then executes the action on the selected text, anywhere in the design mode web page, if it is applicable, usually it is if on a page in design mode.

```
<iframe id="content-iframe" style='border:solid blue;background: white;height: 200px;width: 400px'
src="about:blank"></iframe>
```

This iframe hosts the editable content we could load any web page inside it in design mode but we will be loading a blank page for the purpose of our example.

```
<div id="source" style='border:solid green;background: white;height: 400px;width: 400px' ></div>
```

This div will be used to display the html source code of the editable div contents.

```
var editor;

    function onload() {
        editor = document.getElementById("content-iframe");
        editor.contentDocument.designMode = "on";
    }
window.addEventListener("load", onload, false);
```

The above code creates a variable 'editor' which will store the reference to the iframe with the id 'content-iframe'. It also hooks the 'onload' function to the window 'load' event. The onload function stores the reference to the iframe in the editor variable and sets its design mode 'on'.

```
    function doShowHTML() {
        var bodysource = editor.contentDocument.body.innerHTML;
        bodysource.replace(/</g, '&lt;');
        bodysource.replace(/>/g, '&gt;');
        $('#source').text(bodysource);
    }
```

The doShowHTML function gets the html contents of the editable iframe. It does a global replacement of '<' and '>' characters with '<' and '>' so that they don't get deleted when being shown as text in the 'source' div. It then sets the html snippet as text in the div with the id 'source'

```
function doInsertLink() {
   var url = prompt("URL:", "http://");
   if (url)
      editor.contentDocument.execCommand("createlink", false, url);
}
```

The above function prompts the user for a URL and then calls the contentDocument.execCommand on the iframe passing 'createlink' action and the user entered URL as the parameter. This will be applied to the current selection inside the iframe.

```
function doInsertTable() {
   var size = prompt("Enter desired rows and columns: (rows|cols)", "2|2");
   if (size) {
      var rowcol = size.split("|");
      if (rowcol.length == 2 && rowcol[0] > 0 && rowcol[0] < 10 && rowcol[1] > 0 && rowcol[1] < 10) {
         var html = "<table border='1'>";
         for (var row = 0; row < rowcol[0]; row++) {
            html += "<tr>";
            for (var col = 0; col < rowcol[1]; col++) {
               html += "<td width='20'></td>";
            }
            html += "</tr>";
         }
         html += "</table>";
         editor.contentDocument.execCommand('inserthtml', false, html);
      }
   }
}
```

The above function prompts the user to enter the number of rows and columns in the table. It generates a string snippet of the html of the table to be inserted. And then calls the contentDocument.execCommand on the iframe passing 'inserthtml' as action and the string html snippet as the parameter.

We are all set. Let's take this for a spin in the various browsers. We will be entering 'Hello World' in the editable iframe and making the word World bold. And we will click the View Source button.

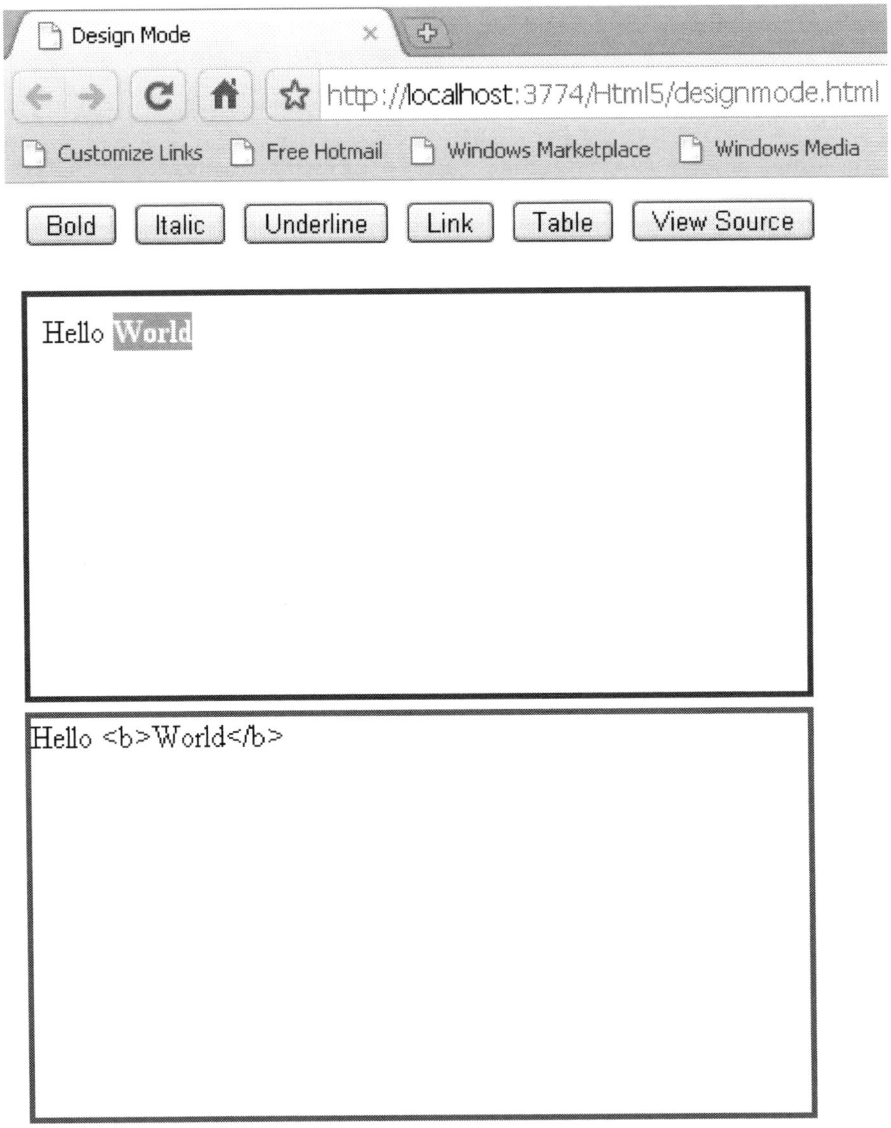

Figure 28 - DesignMode Works in Chrome

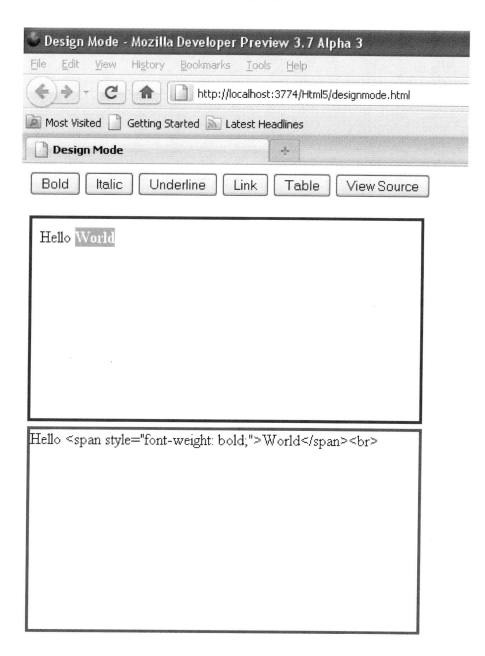

Figure 29 - DesignMode Works in Firefox

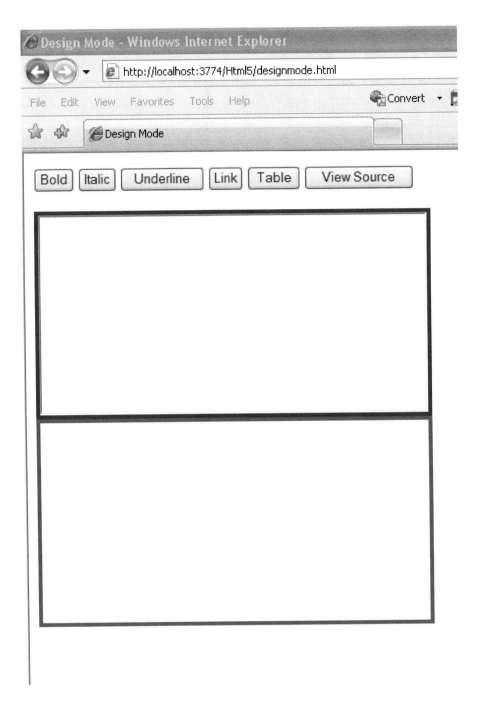

Figure 30 - DesignMode Doesn't Work in IE

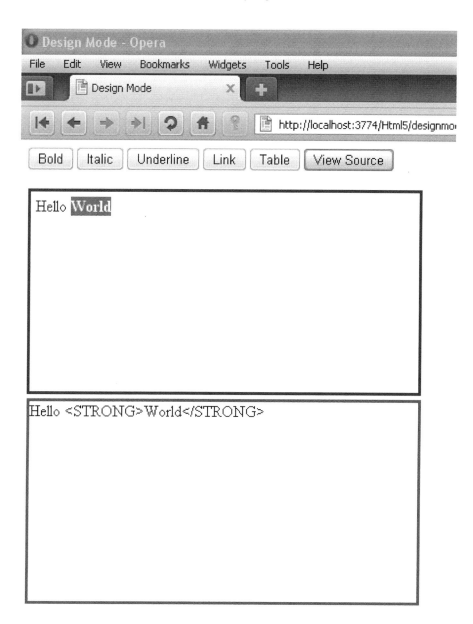

Figure 31 - DesignMode Works in Opera

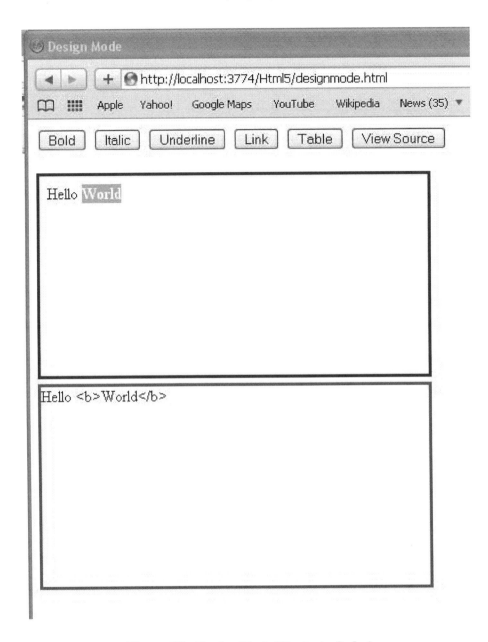

Figure 32 - DesignMode Works in Safari

If you note the generated HTML source is different in different browsers.

A Quick Walkthrough of the Specifications

The 'contentEditable' attribute works with any element and goes along with the 'isContentEditable' attribute as follows

- element.contentEditable [= value] - Value is "true", "false", or "inherit". The last option to inherit the attribute from the containing element

- element.isContentEditable - Returns true if the element is editable; otherwise, returns false.

The designMode attribute of a document is to be used as follows

document.designMode [= value] - Returns "on" if the document is editable, and "off" if it isn't. Can be set, to change the document's current state.

The other relevant API's are as follows

- document.execCommand - Executes the given command.

- document.queryCommandEnabled - Determines whether the given command can be executed on the document in its current state.

- document.queryCommandIndeterm - Determines whether the current selection is in an indetermined state.

- document.queryCommandState - Determines whether the given command has been executed on the current selection.

- document.queryCommandValue - Determines the current value of the document, range, or current selection for the given command.

Document.execCommand executes a command on the current document, current selection, or the given range.

bSuccess = object.execCommand(sCommand [, bUserInterface] [, vValue])

sCommand - Required. String that specifies the command to execute. This command can be any of the command identifiers that can be executed in script.

bUserInterface - Optional. Boolean that specifies one of the following values.

- False - Default. Do not display a user interface. Must be combined with vValue, if the command requires a value.

- True - Display a user interface if the command supports one.

vValue   Optional. Variant that specifies the string, number, or other value to assign. Possible values depend on the command.

Retrospective

We saw the document designmode feature which enables the entire document to be edited. We also tried the contenteditable attribute on a div enabling us to edit its contents. We have not covered the element.spellcheck attribute which is left as an exercise to the user.

Chapter 6- Cross Document/Domain Messaging

HTML 5 allows for messaging across documents both on the same domain and across domains. We are going to illustrate this with a parent page communicating with a child page in an iframe.

Let's get started with the example by creating an html file called 'messaging_parent.html' with the following contents.

```
messaging_parent Code

<!DOCTYPE html>

<html>
<head>
<meta charset="utf-8">
<title>Messaging Parent</title>
<script type="text/javascript" charset="utf-8" src="js/jquery-1.3.2.js"></script>

<script type="text/javascript">

    function dispatchmessage() {
      var message = $("#message").val();
      var loc = window.location;
      var protocol = loc.protocol;
      var host = loc.host;
      // if calling cross domain pass the protocol and host of the CALLED iframe
      document.getElementById("messagediframe").contentWindow.postMessage(message,
protocol+"//"+host);
    }
</script>
</head>
<body>
<section id="wrapper">
  <header>
   <h1>Messaging Parent</h1>
  </header>
<article>
  Message <input id="message" type="text"/><input type="button"  onclick="dispatchmessage();"
value="Dispatch" /><br />
  <iframe id="messagediframe" src="messaging_child.html" height="600" width="800">
  </iframe>
</article>
</section>
</body>
</html>
```

```
function dispatchmessage() {
    var message = $("#message").val();
    var loc = window.location;
    var protocol = loc.protocol;
    var host = loc.host;
    // if calling cross domain pass the protocol and host of the CALLED iframe
    document.getElementById("messagediframe").contentWindow.postMessage(message,
protocol+"//"+host);
    }
```

The 'dispatchmessage' function sends a message to the iframe window. The user enters the message in an input text box with the id 'message'. The important thing to note that along with the message you have to pass another second parameter which should be like '<protocol>//<host>' where protocol is something like 'http:' or 'https:' and host is your web server host including the port if other than 80 e.g. 'localhost:2584'. If the protocol and host doesn't match the one of the called page a security exception is thrown. For a page on the same domain we recover the current window location and retrieve the protocol and host from it and send it as the second paremeter which works because both the pages share the same value only the page url is different. When it comes to messaging a window on a different domain such as 'http://sun.com' we should send the protocol and host of the called page. This results in cross domain messaging. This function will send a message to the iframe on the page with the id 'messagediframe'

```
Message <input id="message" type="text"/><input type="button"  onclick="dispatchmessage();"
value="Dispatch" /><br />
```

This code renders an input text box which will be used to fetch the message from the user. It also renders a button which when clicked will call the 'dispatchmessage' function which will dispatch the message to the iframe.

```
<iframe id="messagediframe" src="messaging_child.html" height="600" width="800">
</iframe>
```

This iframe contains the called page 'messaging_child.html' which will receive the message.

Let's create the 'messaging_child.html' page with the following contents.

```
messaging_child.html Code

<!DOCTYPE html>

<html>
<head>
<meta charset="utf-8">
<title>Messaging Child</title>
<script type="text/javascript" charset="utf-8" src="js/jquery-1.3.2.js"></script>

<script type="text/javascript">

   onmessage = function (e) {
     //if (e.origin !="..."){...}
     $("#messages").html($("#messages").html() + e.data + "</br>");
   }
</script>

</head>
<body>
<section id="wrapper">
  <header>
    <h1>Messaging Child</h1>
  </header>
<article>
  <div id="messages"  style="width:400px; height:400px; border:dotted blue;background:
white"></div>
</article>
</section>
</body>
</html>
```

This page has one div which will display the received message(s).

```
<div id="messages"  style="width:400px; height:400px; border:dotted blue;background: white"></div>
```

The div has an id of 'messages'.

```
onmessage = function (e) {
     //if (e.origin !="..."){...}
     $("#messages").html($("#messages").html() + e.data + "</br>");
```

```
}
```

The above code hooks the function to the page's onmessage event as its handler. It recovers the message payload from the data attribute of the event variable 'e'. It then appends the message to the div with the id 'messages'

We are all set. Let's try the example out in various browsers. We shall enter the message 'Hello World' in the text box and hit the 'Dispatch' button.

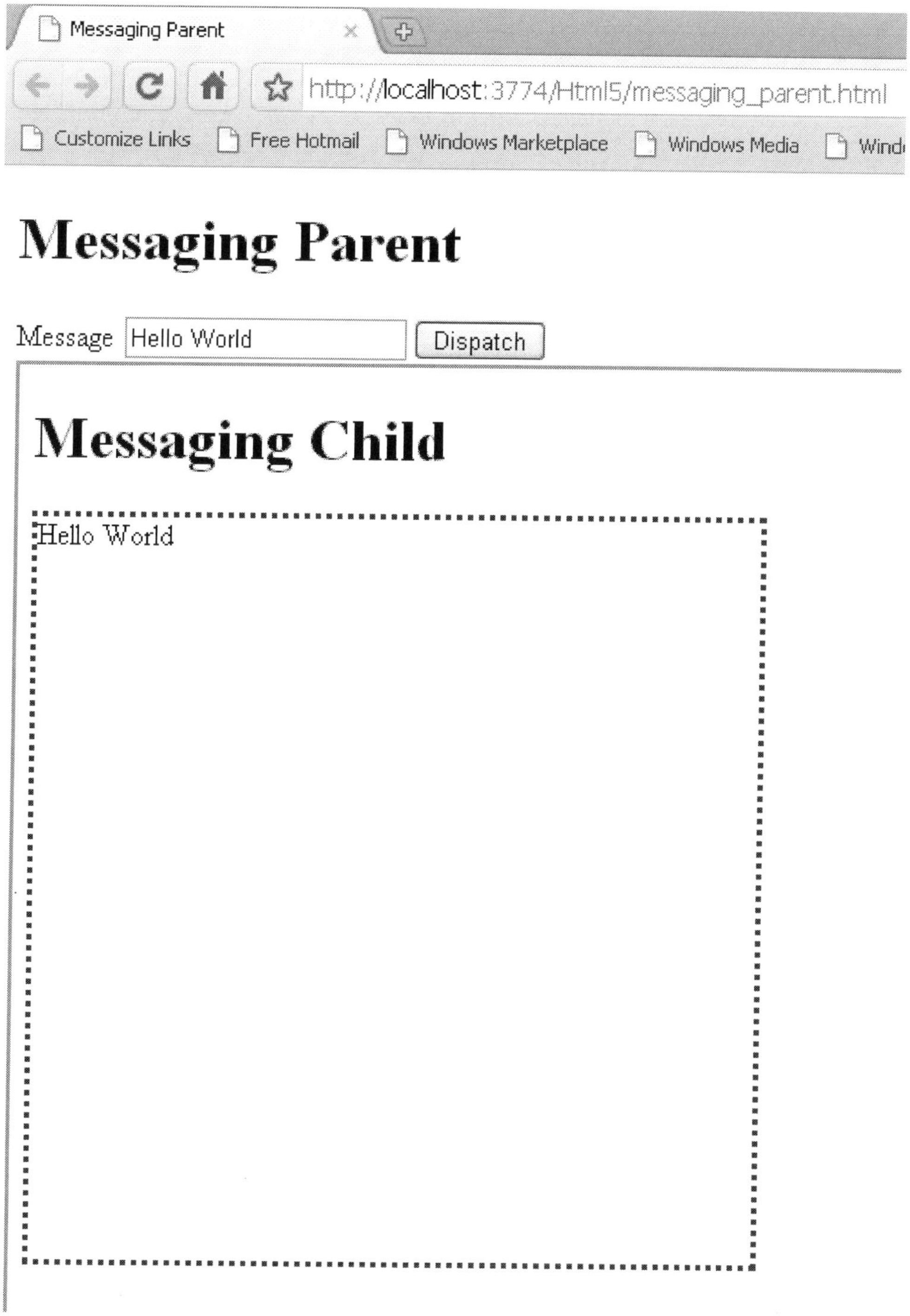

Figure 33 - Cross Document Messaging Works in Chrome

Figure 34 - Cross Document Messaging Doesn't Work in Firefox

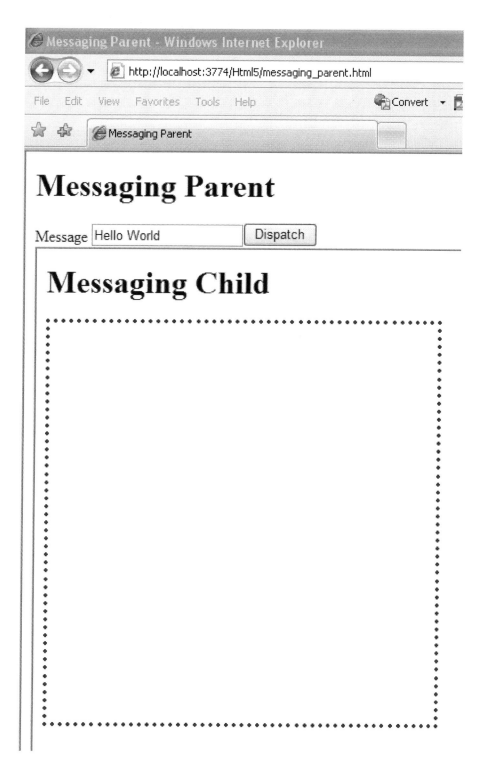

Figure 35 - Cross Document Messaging Doesn't Work in IE

Messaging Parent

Message [Hello World] [Dispatch]

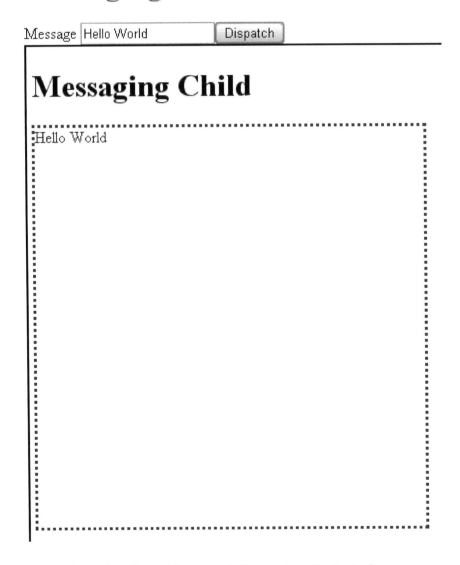

Figure 36 - Cross Document Messaging Works in Opera

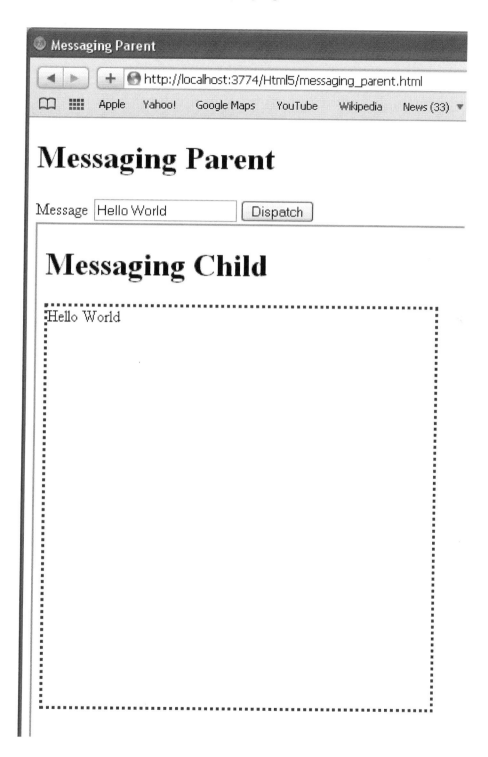

Figure 37 - Cross Document Messaging Works in Safari

A Quick Walkthrough of the Specifications

The event object has the following attributes

event.data - Returns the data of the message.

event.origin - Returns the origin of the message.

event.source - Returns the WindowProxy of the source window.

event.ports - Returns the MessagePortArray sent with the message.

event.lastEventId – is used only with Server Sent Events

The window.onmessage event is used to receive the events

```
window.addEventListener('message', receiver, false);
function receiver(e) {
  if (e.origin == 'http://example.com') {
    if (e.data == 'Hello world') {
      e.source.postMessage('Hello', e.origin);
    } else {
      alert(e.data);
    }
  }
}
```

The event handler should check the origin of the events to make sure they are allowed to send messages to the window where e.origin refers to the domain which the source page has been loaded from and e.source points to the source Window which allows for two way communication. The Sending window sends message using code similar to the following code.

```
var o = document.getElementsByTagName('iframe')[0];
o.contentWindow.postMessage('Hello world', 'http://b.example.org/');
```

Channel Messaging

Between pages HTML 5 also supports channel messaging which are implemented as two-way pipes with ports at each end. You send and receive messages from one port and pass the other port for use by the other window.

```
var channel = new MessageChannel();
```

The above statement constructs a channel. The statement below sends the handshake message with the port for future communication to the target window.

```
targetWindow.postMessage('take the port and use it to receive my future messages and to send messages back to me...', 'http://example.com', channel.port2);
```

The target window receives the handshake message, and hooks onto the port message event, sent across using code like below.

```
var portToTheSourceWindow;

window.addEventListener('message', receiver, false);
function receiver(e) {
  portToTheSourceWindow = e.ports[0];
  portToTheSourceWindow.onmessage = handleMessage;
}

function handleMessage(event) {
  alert( event.data );
}
```

To send messages the postMessage method is used on the channel's source side port i.e. port1 in our case.

```
channel.port1.postMessage('this is my message');
```

To receive messages source window event handers listens on the message events of the source window side port i.e. port1 in our case.

```
channel.port1.onmessage = handleMessage;
function handleMessage(event) {
  alert( event.data );
}
```

Retrospective

We created two html pages i.e. parent and child and we sent messages from the parent to the child. Cross Document Messaging will work across domains. A feature which was not possible earlier due to Cross Site Scripting restrictions in browsers not allowing messages to be sent to other windows of other domains. We didn't try out the Message Channels feature of Cross Document Messaging which will allow our applications to create multiple channels for messaging between windows for different purposes instead of all the messages passing to and fro from the default mechanism. Which is left as an exercise to the reader.

Chapter 7- Offline Applications

HTML 5 presents the possibility of creating offline applications. It does so in two ways by allowing resources to be cached on the client's browser and by providing a client side SQL database (Web Database) to store data when the browser is offline. For these to work we have to cache the login credentials and provide access to the application in offline mode. We shall cover the two features without delving into offline authentication as that's not HTML 5 specific.

Let's create the manifest file which tells HTML 5 browsers which files can be cached on the browser and which one's need to be loaded from the network only.

HTML 5 Manifest file code

```
CACHE MANIFEST
# v1

# always loaded from the cache
js/jquery-1.3.2.js

# This is a fallback.
FALLBACK:
jpg/ jpg/cartoon-baby.jpg


# Always loaded from the network
NETWORK:
/media
```

The first line states this is the cache manifest. Followed by all items that are loaded from the cache, which in our case is just one JQuery javascript library. Then we have a fallback section which states which file to default to in case there is an error retrieving a file or files on a certain path. And finally the network section which states which file(s)/path(s) need to be always loaded from the network.

Let's create a small page with a cached image on it as follows.

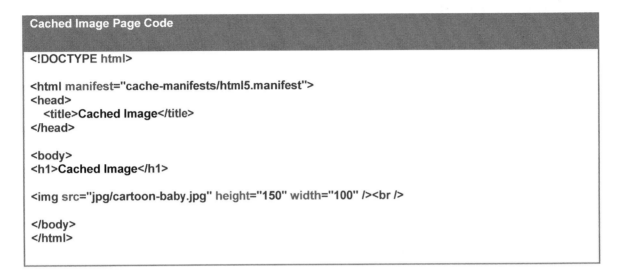

```
Cached Image Page Code

<!DOCTYPE html>

<html manifest="cache-manifests/html5.manifest">
<head>
   <title>Cached Image</title>
</head>

<body>
<h1>Cached Image</h1>

<img src="jpg/cartoon-baby.jpg" height="150" width="100" /><br />

</body>
</html>
```

The important thing to note here is the manifest attribute in the 'html' tag which is a new feature of HTML 5. This attribute links the manifest file to the page, every page could have its own manifest file or there could be one on the homepage/login-page.

When we open the page in firefox it prompts us for permission to use the cache.

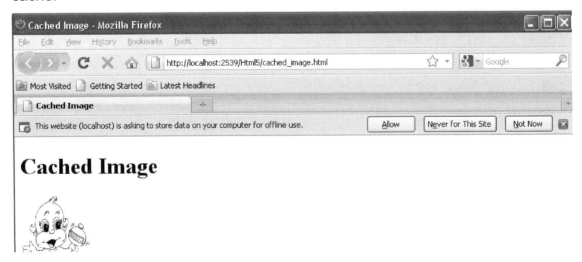

Figure 38 - Firefox Prompts for Permission to Use the Cache

Let's quickly try out the cache feature in other browsers.

Cached Image

Figure 39 - Chrome Ignores the Cache Manifest

Figure 40 - IE Ignores the Cache Manifest

Figure 41 - Opera Ignores the Cache Manifest

Figure 42 - Safari Ignores the Cache Manifest

The other mechanism for offline applications is through the use of client side SQL database. Let's quickly go through that.

```
Client Side SQL Database Code

<!DOCTYPE html>

<html>
<head>
  <meta http-equiv="Content-Type" content="text/html; charset=ISO-8859-1">
  <title>Offline Apps</title>
  <script type="text/javascript" charset="utf-8" src="js/jquery-1.3.2.js"></script>
  <script type="text/javascript" charset="utf-8" src="js/json2.js"></script>


  <script type="text/javascript">
    var db;

    $(document).ready(function () {
      db = openDatabase('emaildatabase', '1.0', 'Email Database', 10240);

      $(window).bind('online', function () {
        alert('We are online. Syncing Offline Data with Server...');
```

```
        });

    $(window).bind('offline', function () {
        alert('We are offline. Will save all data to Local Database');
    });
}

function renderemail(row) {
    // renders the email
    var rowString = "<tr style='border:solid blue;background: white'><td><input id='" +
row['name'] + "' type='checkbox'></input></td><td>" + row['name'] + "</td><td>" + row['email'] +
"</td></tr>";
    $('#emailtable tr:last').after(rowString);
}
function reportError(source, message) {
    $("#emailtable").html("<b>" + source + "</b>:" + message);
}

function reloademails() {
    db.transaction(function (tx) {
        tx.executeSql('CREATE TABLE IF NOT EXISTS Emails(name TEXT, email TEXT)',
        []);
        tx.executeSql('SELECT * FROM Emails', [], function (tx, rs) {
            var rows = rs.rows;
            $("#emailtable tr:gt(0)").remove();
            for (var i = 0; i < rows.length; i++) {
                renderemail(rows.item(i));
            }
        });
    });
}

function insertemail() {
    var name = $("#Name").val();
    var email = $("#Email").val();

    db.transaction(function (tx) {
        tx.executeSql('INSERT INTO Emails VALUES(?, ?)', [name, email],
        function (tx, rs) {
            reloademails();
        },
        function (tx, error) {
            reportError('sql', error.message);
        });
    });
}

function deleteemail(name) {
    db.transaction(function (tx) {
        tx.executeSql('DELETE FROM Emails WHERE name=?', [name],
        function (tx, rs) {
            reloademails();
        },
        function (tx, error) {
            reportError('sql', error.message);
```

```
            });
          });
      }


      function deleteselectedemails() {
        $('#emailtable input:checked').each(function () {
          var name = this.id;
          deleteemail(name);
        });
        reloademails();
      }


  </script>
</head>
<body>
<div>
    <h1>Emails</h1>
    <button onclick="reloademails();">Reload</button><button
onclick="deleteselectedemails();">Delete Selected Emails</button><br/>
    <div id="error"></div><br />
    <table id="emailtable" border="1">
        <tr style='border:dotted blue;background: white'>
          <th>Select</th>
          <th>Name</th>
          <th>Email</th>
        </tr>

    </table>
    <h1>Add an Email</h1>
    Name <input id="Name" type="text"/><br />
    Email <input id="Email" type="text"/><br />
    <button id="insertemailbutton" onclick='insertemail();'>Insert Email</button><br />

  </div>
</body>
</html>
```

```
<button onclick="reloademails();">Reload</button><button onclick="deleteselectedemails();">Delete
Selected Emails</button><br/>
```

Two buttons are being rendered here one to 'Reload' the list and the other to 'Delete Selected Emails' they call the 'reloademails' and 'deleteselectedemails' functions respectively.

```
<div id="error"></div><br />
```

This div is meant to render error messages if any.

```
<table id="emailtable" border="1">
    <tr style='border:dotted blue;background: white'>
        <th>Select</th>
        <th>Name</th>
        <th>Email</th>
    </tr>
</table>
```

This is the table which contains all the email addresses. Has three columns the first one for the checkbox followed by 'name' and 'email'.

```
<h1>Add an Email</h1>
Name <input id="Name" type="text"/><br />
Email <input id="Email" type="text"/><br />
<button id="insertemailbutton" onclick='insertemail();'>Insert Email</button><br />
```

This section is used to add an email address to the list. It has two text boxes one each for Name and Email and then it has a button to Insert Email which calls the 'insertemail' function.

```
var db;
```

The 'db' variable is a global variable that stores a reference to the database.

```
$(document).ready(function () {
        db = openDatabase('emaildatabase', '1.0', 'Email Database', 10240);

        $(window).bind('online', function () {
            alert('We are online. Syncing Offline Data with Server...');
        });

        $(window).bind('offline', function () {
            alert('We are offline. Will save all data to Local Database');
        });
}
```

This function gets called when the document is ready. It opens a connection to the database with the name 'emaildatabase'. Note you don't have to specifically create a database. The version number is 1.0 followed by the database name and size.

Then the method binds to two events 'online' and 'offline'. This is done so that when the page is offline we should put in logic to use the client side db and when it's online we should sync the client db with the server, and use the server instead of the client side db. As of now it simply alerts the status.

```
function renderemail(row) {
            // renders the email
            var rowString = "<tr style='border:solid blue;background:
white'><td><input id='" + row['name'] + "' type='checkbox'></input></td><td>" +
row['name'] + "</td><td>" + row['email'] + "</td></tr>";
            $('#emailtable tr:last').after(rowString);
}

function reportError(source, message) {
    $("#emailtable").html("<b>" + source + "</b>:" + message);
}


    function reloademails() {
        db.transaction(function (tx) {
            tx.executeSql('CREATE TABLE IF NOT EXISTS Emails(name TEXT, email
TEXT)',
            []);
            tx.executeSql('SELECT * FROM Emails', [], function (tx, rs) {
                var rows = rs.rows;
                $("#emailtable tr:gt(0)").remove();
                for (var i = 0; i < rows.length; i++) {
                    renderemail(rows.item(i));
                }
            });
        });
    }
```

The above code is used to reload the emails. The main function here is reload emails, the renderemail and reproterror functions are helper functions.

The 'reloademails' function starts a db transaction with a callback function. Which creates the 'Emails' table with 'name' and 'email' TEXT columns, if the table doesn't already exist.

Then the function selects all rows from the Emails table. It removes all rows from the 'emailtable' other than the first row. It then loops over each of the rows in the resultset and renders them one by one.by calling the 'renderemail' function.

The renderemail function creates a string with html code using the data row and appends it to the 'emailtable'. The 'reporterror' appends a snippet of html with the error and sets it as the content of the 'error' div.

```
function insertemail() {
    var name = $("#Name").val();
    var email = $("#Email").val();

    db.transaction(function (tx) {
      tx.executeSql('INSERT INTO Emails VALUES(?, ?)', [name, email],
      function (tx, rs) {
        reloademails();
      },
      function (tx, error) {
        reportError('sql', error.message);
      });
    });
  }
```

The 'insertemail' function gets the 'Name' and 'Email' values from their respective textboxes and starts a transaction. It then inserts the values into the 'Emails' table. After the SQL gets executes it calls 'reloademails' using the callback mechanism. And also calls 'reportError' function in case an error is encountered.

```
function deleteemail(name) {
        db.transaction(function (tx) {
          tx.executeSql('DELETE FROM Emails WHERE name=?', [name],
          function (tx, rs) {
            reloademails();
          },
          function (tx, error) {
            reportError('sql', error.message);
```

```
        });
      });
   }
```

The 'deleteemail' function starts a transaction and deletes the email from the 'Emails' table where the name matches the name in the selected email to be deleted. It then calls 'reloademails' which refreshes the list and the reportError method in case errors are encountered.

```
function deleteselectedemails() {
      $('#emailtable input:checked').each(function () {
         var name = this.id;
         deleteemail(name);
      });
      reloademails();
   }
```

This method gets called when the 'Delete Emails' button is pressed. It selects all rows in the table with the checkbox checked and for each of those rows it fetches the 'id' of the checkbox (it contains the 'name') and then it calls the 'deleteemail' function.

Let's see it in action.

Figure 43 - Initial Page in Opera

The first thing we do is to click 'Reload' as it contains the script to create the table. Next let's try and insert a record into the table.

Emails

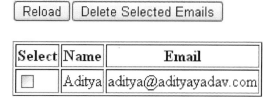

Add an Email

Figure 44 - Inserting a Record

Now let's check the checkbox and click 'Delete Selected Emails'

Figure 45 - The Email Gets Deleted

Now let's try 'Reload' and then inserting email in the other browsers.

Figure 46 - Everything Works in Safari

Figure 47 - Inserting a Record Fails in Firefox

The client side db feature is not implemented in Firefox.

Figure 48 - Inserting a Record Fails in Chrome

The client side db feature is not implemented in Chrome.

Figure 49 - Inserting a Record Fails in IE

The client side db feature is not implemented in IE.

A Quick Walkthrough of the Specifications

In order for users to continue using applications without a network connection HTML 5 allows the developer to declare using a cache manifest files which are needed to run the web page without an internet connection, i.e. which files the browser needs to cache so that it can be used offline.

```
CACHE MANIFEST
NETWORK:
comm.cgi
CACHE:
style/default.css
images/sound-icon.png
images/background.png
```

The above example states that the comm.cgi script is whitelisted and will always be loaded from the network. The css and png files listed will always be cached.

```
CACHE MANIFEST
FALLBACK:
/ /offline.html
NETWORK:
*
```

The above manifest defines a catch all fallback page offline.html which will get displayed instead of any page when the user is offline. It says that everything will be loaded from the network '*'

```
CACHE: - Switches to the explicit section.
FALLBACK: - Switches to the fallback section.
NETWORK: - Switches to the online whitelist section.
```

There are three possible network headers as shown above.

cache = window.applicationCache - (In a window.) Returns the ApplicationCache object that applies to the active document of that Window.

cache.status - Returns the current status of the application cache, e.g. UNCACHED, IDLE, CHECKING, DOWNLOADING, UPDATEREADY, and OBSOLETE

cache.update() - Invokes the application cache download process. Throws an INVALID_STATE_ERR exception if there is no application cache to update.

cache.swapCache() - Switches to the most recent application cache, if there is a newer one. If there isn't, throws an INVALID_STATE_ERR exception.

The cache object supports the following events

```
onchecking
```

onerror

onnoupdate

ondownloading

onprogress

onupdateready

oncached

onobsolete

window . navigator . online - Returns false if the user agent is definitely offline (disconnected from the network). Returns true if the user agent might be online.

The openDatabase method on the Window and WorkerUtils interfaces and the openDatabaseSync method on the WorkerUtils interface take the following arguments: a database name, a database version, a display name, an estimated size in bytes of the data that will be stored in the database and a callback to be invoked if the database has not yet been created.

The rest of the specification ends adruptly with a reference to SQLite being the implementation and hence everything that works in SQLite should work with the client side database feature.

Retrospective

In this chapter we saw two things that were essential to create an offline application i.e. a way to cache resources for offline use and a way to use a SQLite client side db when the network is not available. The exact algorithm for syncing local changes with the server was not included in the example which is left as an exercise to the user.

Chapter 8- Audio & Video

Converting Audio & Video into Ogg format using Ffmpeg

Let's record a desktop video using Windows Media Encoder and convert it to Ogg format for use in HTML 5 web applications. Download and install Windows Media Encoder from the following URL http://www.microsoft.com/windows/windowsmedia/download/AllDownloads.aspx

Install it and start it and select the 'Capture Screen' Option and click ok. Start Internet Explorer, we will use it to search for 'Aditya Yadav & Associates' and visit the homepage and record it as a video named as 'WMESampleVideo.wmv'.

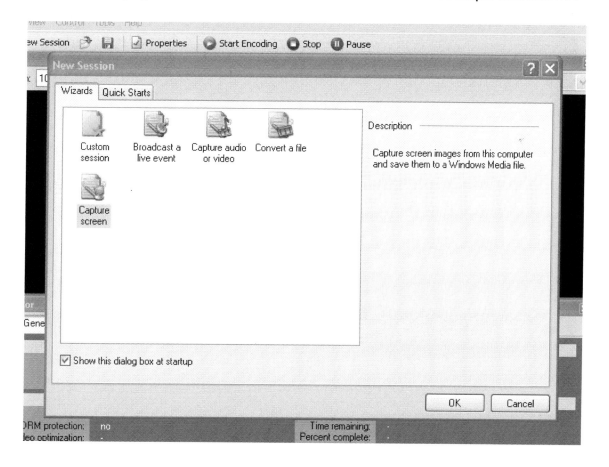

Figure 50 - Choose Capture Screen Option

On the next page choose the 'Specific Window' option and click ok.

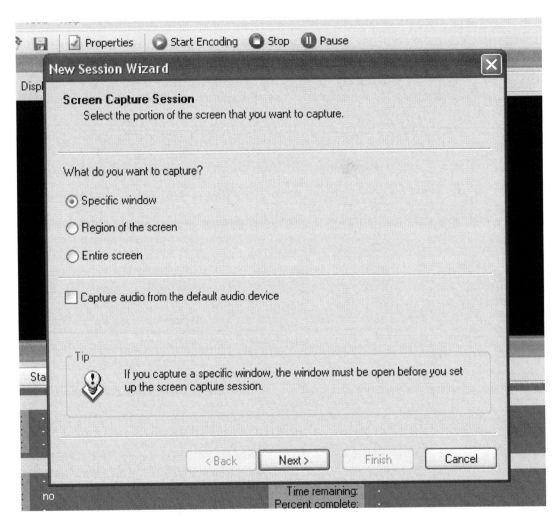

Figure 51 - Choose Specific Window Option

On the next screen select the IE Window, it will have the name of the web page title it is displaying currently.

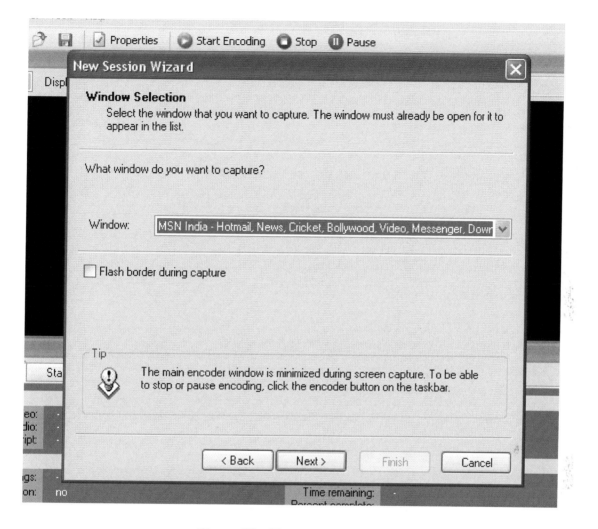

Figure 52 - Choose the IE Window

On the next screen browse to the location and enter a filename for the video that we will create e.g. Desktop and 'WMESampleVideo.wmv'

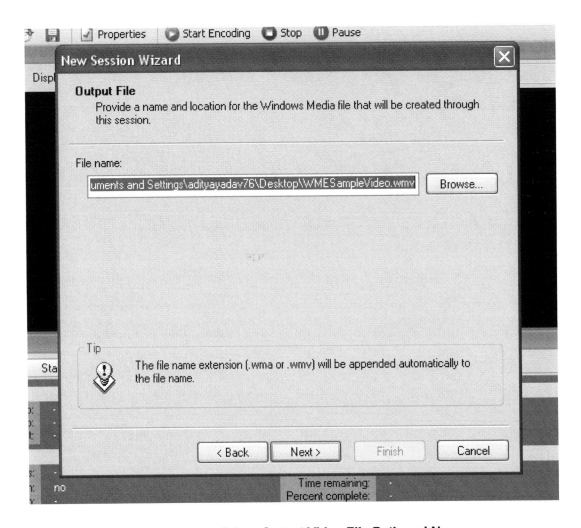

Figure 53 - Select Output Video File Path and Name

On the next screen select the 'High' quality settings.

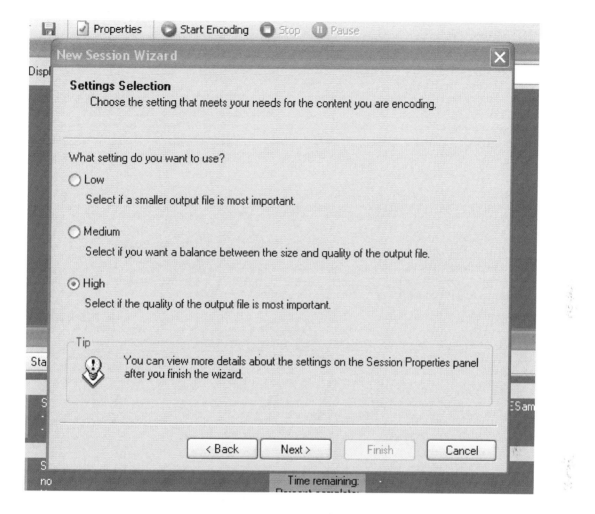

Figure 54 - Choose the High Quality Settings

On the next screen click Finish button. Click Properties button on the toolbar. Select the Compression Tab. Click the 'Edit...' button and select the 'Windows Media Video 9' codec.

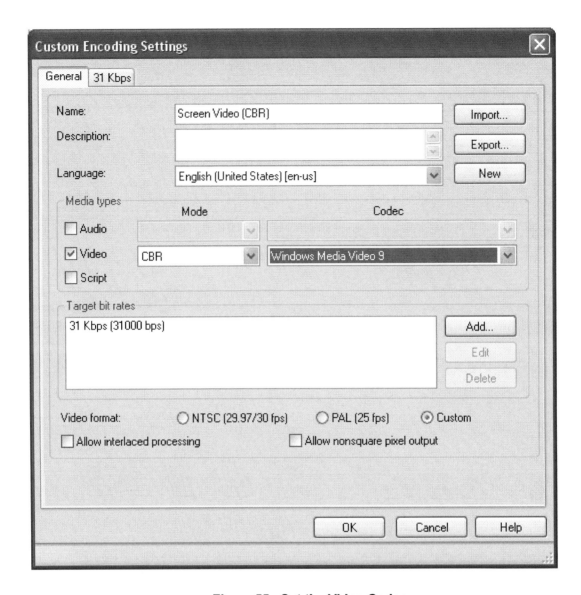

Figure 55 - Set the Video Codec

Close all wizards. And on the main window click 'Start Encoding'. Proceed to enter google.com in IE. On the google search text box enter 'Aditya Yadav & Associates' and hit search. Then click on the AY&A homepage. Go back to the Windows Media Encoder and stop the video capture.

We will use FFMpeg to encode the video into Ogg format. You can find the FFMpeg.exe executable in the source bundle accompanying this book or you can download it for windows from http://www.videohelp.com/tools/ffmpeg.

Use notepad to create a file named 'Convert.bat' file with the following line

```
ffmpeg -i %1 -vcodec libtheora -sameq -acodec libvorbis -ac 2 -sameq %2
```

This batch file will take 2 parameters the first one will be the name of the source file which is to be converted and the second parameter will be the name of the output file typically <something.ogg>. This batch file calls the ffmpeg executable and sets the video codec to theora, the audio codec to vorbis, 2 channel audio output and to maintain the same quality in the encoding as present in the source file.

Use the command: convert.bat WMESampleVideo.flv WMESampleVideo.ogg

This will take about 20 minutes to convert.

```
Console Output: Encoding a WMV output from WME into Ogg

G:\workspace>convert WMESampleVideo.wmv WMESampleVideo.ogg

G:\workspace>ffmpeg -i WMESamp
leVideo.wmv -vcodec libtheora -sameq -acodec libvorbis -ac 2 -sameq WMESampleVid
eo.ogg
FFmpeg version SVN-r22140-Sherpya, Copyright (c) 2000-2010 the FFmpeg developers

  built on Mar  2 2010 03:26:44 with gcc 4.2.5 20080919 (prerelease) [Sherpya]
  libavutil    50. 9. 0 / 50. 9. 0
  libavcodec   52.55. 0 / 52.55. 0
  libavformat  52.54. 0 / 52.54. 0
  libavdevice  52. 2. 0 / 52. 2. 0
  libavfilter   1.17. 0 / 1.17. 0
  libswscale    0.10. 0 / 0.10. 0
  libpostproc  51. 2. 0 / 51. 2. 0
Input #0, asf, from 'WMESampleVideo.wmv':
  Metadata:
    title       :
    author      :
    copyright   :
    comment     :
```

```
WMFSDKVersion   : 9.00.00.4503
WMFSDKNeeded    : 0.0.0.0000
IsVBR        : 0
Duration: 00:00:32.60, start: 3.000000, bitrate: 250 kb/s
  Stream #0.0(eng): Video: wmv3, yuv420p, 800x600, 250 kb/s, 1k tbr, 1k tbn, 1
k tbc
Output #0, ogg, to 'WMESampleVideo.ogg':
 Metadata:
  encoder        : Lavf52.54.0
  Stream #0.0(eng): Video: libtheora, yuv420p, 800x600, q=2-31, 200 kb/s, 1k t
bn, 1k tbc
Stream mapping:
  Stream #0.0 -> #0.0
Press [q] to stop encoding
frame=  75 fps= 25 q=0.0 size=  190kB time=0.07 bitrate=20732.4kbits/s dup=7
frame= 130 fps= 25 q=0.0 size=  297kB time=0.12 bitrate=19432.2kbits/s dup=1
frame= 196 fps= 26 q=0.0 size=  456kB time=0.20 bitrate=19039.9kbits/s dup=1
frame= 265 fps= 26 q=0.0 size=  590kB time=0.27 bitrate=18247.3kbits/s dup=2
frame= 329 fps= 11 q=0.0 size=  752kB time=0.33 bitrate=18713.9kbits/s dup=3
frame= 396 fps= 12 q=0.0 size=  887kB time=0.40 bitrate=18340.1kbits/s dup=3
frame= 474 fps= 13 q=0.0 size= 1076kB time=0.47 bitrate=18596.1kbits/s dup=4
frame= 525 fps= 13 q=0.0 size= 1184kB time=0.53 bitrate=18481.5kbits/s dup=5
frame= 594 fps= 14 q=0.0 size= 1346kB time=0.59 bitrate=18569.2kbits/s dup=5
frame= 659 fps= 11 q=0.0 size= 1483kB time=0.66 bitrate=18438.8kbits/s dup=6
frame= 723 fps= 11 q=0.0 size= 1647kB time=0.72 bitrate=18658.4kbits/s dup=7
frame= 789 fps= 12 q=0.0 size= 1800kB time=0.79 bitrate=18691.7kbits/s dup=7
frame= 855 fps= 12 q=0.0 size= 1982kB time=0.85 bitrate=18991.3kbits/s dup=8
frame= 921 fps= 13 q=0.0 size= 2134kB time=0.92 bitrate=18981.4kbits/s dup=9
frame= 987 fps= 11 q=0.0 size= 2316kB time=0.99 bitrate=19219.2kbits/s dup=9
frame= 1053 fps= 11 q=0.0 size=  2468kB time=1.05 bitrate=19199.0kbits/s dup=1
frame= 1119 fps= 11 q=0.0 size=  2650kB time=1.12 bitrate=19398.8kbits/s dup=1
frame= 1184 fps= 11 q=0.0 size=  2802kB time=1.18 bitrate=19387.9kbits/s dup=1
frame= 1253 fps= 12 q=0.0 size=  2985kB time=1.25 bitrate=19514.4kbits/s dup=1
frame= 1317 fps= 12 q=0.0 size=  3138kB time=1.32 bitrate=19517.2kbits/s dup=1
  .
  .
  .
frame=32212 fps= 12 q=0.0 size=  67537kB time=32.21 bitrate=17175.6kbits/s dup=
frame=32271 fps= 12 q=0.0 size=  67633kB time=32.27 bitrate=17168.6kbits/s dup=
frame=32337 fps= 13 q=0.0 size=  67729kB time=32.34 bitrate=17158.0kbits/s dup=
frame=32406 fps= 13 q=0.0 size=  67844kB time=32.41 bitrate=17150.6kbits/s dup=
frame=32470 fps= 12 q=0.0 size=  67941kB time=32.47 bitrate=17141.1kbits/s dup=
frame=32536 fps= 12 q=0.0 size=  68056kB time=32.54 bitrate=17135.2kbits/s dup=
frame=32536 fps= 12 q=0.0 Lsize=  68056kB time=32.54 bitrate=17135.2kbits/s dup
=32299 drop=0
video:67053kB audio:0kB global headers:3kB muxing overhead 1.490502%
```

This will convert the source file WMESampleVideo.wmv and store the output in WMESampleVideo.ogg. Use the VLC Player (http://www.videolan.org/) to play the ogg file and review the conversion.

Encoding an existing FLV into Ogg

Searching for free sample FLV files on google gives us http://www.mediacollege.com/adobe/flash/video/tutorial/example-flv.html. Lets download one file and convert it into Ogg using the convert batch file we made earlier in this chapter.

Use the command: convert.bat FLVSampleVideo.flv FLVSampleVideo.ogg

```
Console Output: Encoding an existing FLV into Ogg

G:\workspace>convert FLVSampleVideo.flv FLVSampleVideo.ogg

G:\workspace>ffmpeg -i FLVSamp
leVideo.flv -vcodec libtheora -sameq -acodec libvorbis -ac 2 -sameq FLVSampleVid
eo.ogg
FFmpeg version SVN-r22140-Sherpya, Copyright (c) 2000-2010 the FFmpeg developers

  built on Mar  2 2010 03:26:44 with gcc 4.2.5 20080919 (prerelease) [Sherpya]
  libavutil    50. 9. 0 / 50. 9. 0
  libavcodec   52.55. 0 / 52.55. 0
  libavformat  52.54. 0 / 52.54. 0
  libavdevice  52. 2. 0 / 52. 2. 0
  libavfilter   1.17. 0 /  1.17. 0
  libswscale    0.10. 0 /  0.10. 0
  libpostproc  51. 2. 0 / 51. 2. 0
[flv @ 0190d020]Estimating duration from bitrate, this may be inaccurate

Seems stream 0 codec frame rate differs from container frame rate: 1000.00 (1000
/1) -> 25.00 (25/1)
Input #0, flv, from 'FLVSampleVideo.flv':
  Metadata:
    duration       : 17
    width          : 360
    height         : 288
    videodatarate  : 260
    framerate      : 25
    videocodecid   : 4
    audiodatarate  : 40
    audiodelay     : 0
    audiocodecid   : 2
    canSeekToEnd   : 1
    creationdate   : Fri Feb 03 11:52:46 2006

  Duration: 00:00:16.92, start: 0.000000, bitrate: 306 kb/s
    Stream #0.0: Video: vp6f, yuv420p, 360x288, 266 kb/s, 25 tbr, 1k tbn, 1k tbc

    Stream #0.1: Audio: mp3, 22050 Hz, 2 channels, s16, 40 kb/s
File 'FLVSampleVideo.ogg' already exists. Overwrite ? [y/N] y
```

```
Output #0, ogg, to 'FLVSampleVideo.ogg':
  Metadata:
    encoder        : Lavf52.54.0
    Stream #0.0: Video: libtheora, yuv420p, 360x288, q=2-31, 200 kb/s, 25 tbn, 2
5 tbc
    Stream #0.1: Audio: vorbis, 22050 Hz, 2 channels, s16, 64 kb/s
Stream mapping:
  Stream #0.0 -> #0.0
  Stream #0.1 -> #0.1
Press [q] to stop encoding
frame=  424 fps= 63 q=0.0 Lsize=    495kB time=16.95 bitrate= 239.2kbits/s
video:319kB audio:133kB global headers:7kB muxing overhead 7.998441%
```

This will convert the source file FLVSampleVideo.flv and store the output in FLVSampleVideo.ogg. Use the VLC Player to play the ogg file and review the conversion.

Encoding Ogg video using Firefogg plugin for Firefox

Start firefox and open http://www.firefogg.org

Figure 56 - Firefogg Homepage

Click on the Install Firefogg link.

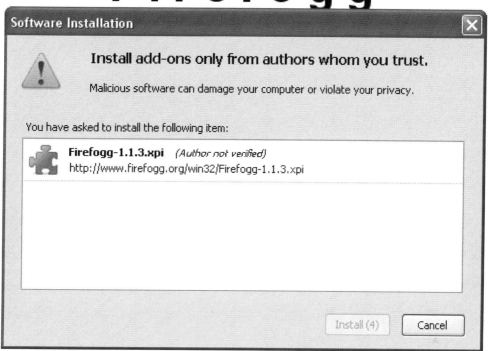

Figure 57 - Installing the Firefogg Plugin

Click on Install Now button. Restart Firefox and click Tools->Make Ogg Video menu.

Figure 58 - Tools -> Make Ogg Video

This launches a new browser window.

Make Ogg Video

Firefogg - video encoding and uploading for Firefox

Sites using Firefogg - Use Firefogg on your Site - Make Ogg Video

☞ Select new file   ⊟ Save Ogg

FLVSampleVideo.flv

▸ **Preset: Web Video Theora, Vorbis 400kbs & 400px max width**

▸ **Encoding range**

▸ **Basic quality and resolution control**

Figure 59 - Select the Source FLV File

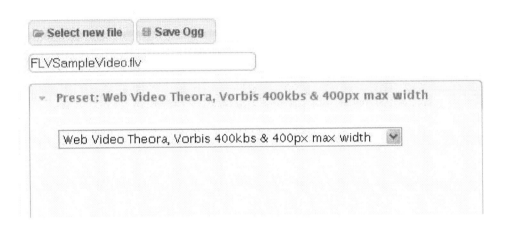

Figure 60 - Select the Preset

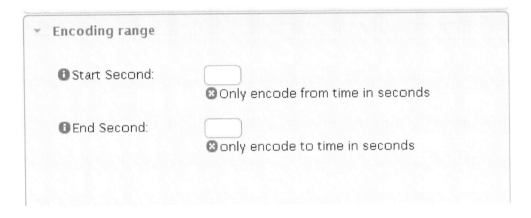

Figure 61 - Select the Ending Range

If you want to limit the enconding to a range within the source file enter the start and/or end time.

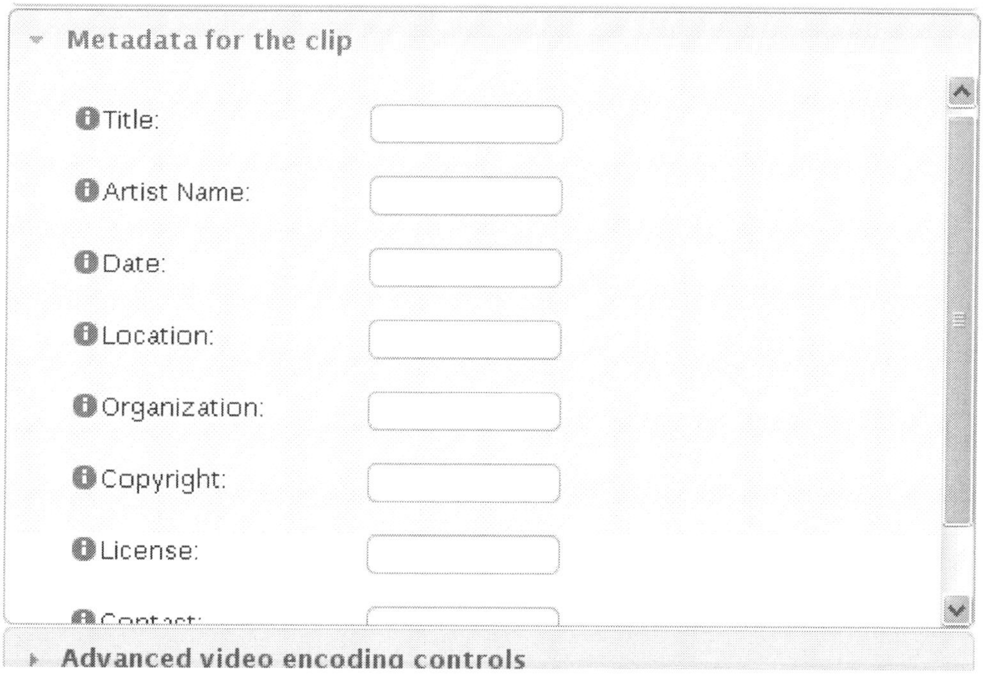

Figure 62 - Enter the Metadata

Figure 63 - Enter Basic Quality and Resolution Controls

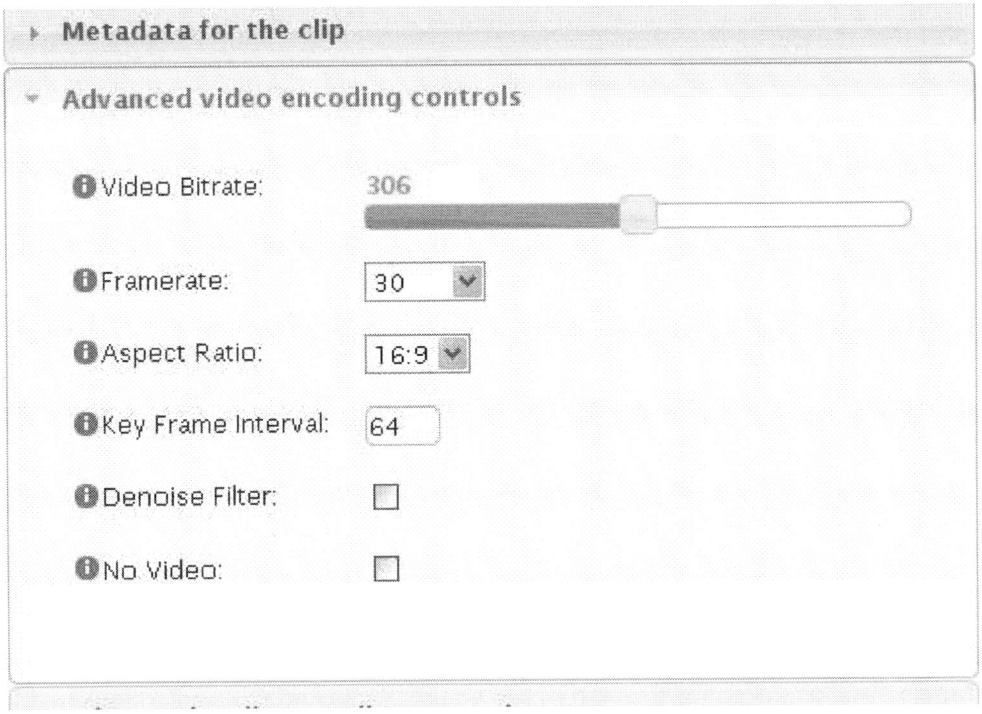

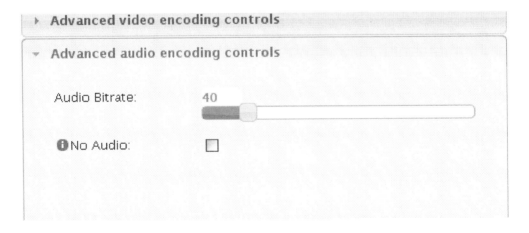

Figure 64 - Enter the Advanced Video Encoding Controls

Figure 65 - Enter the Advanced Audio Encoding Controls

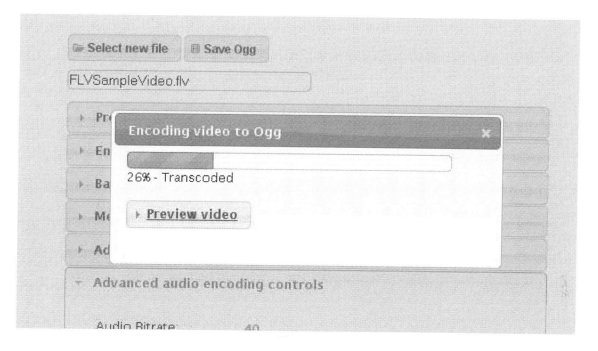

Figure 66 - Click Save to Select Output File and Start Encoding

Figure 67 - Preview the Video after Encoding Finishes

We now have 3 video files with which we will create the Video page in the next section.

Creating the Video page

Create a video page video.html in notepad with the following contents.

```
Video.html page contents

<!DOCTYPE html>

<html>
<head>
<meta charset="utf-8">
<title>Video</title>
</head>
<body>
```

```
<section id="wrapper">
  <header>
   <h1>Video</h1>
  </header>
<article>
  <video controls height="150" width="200" src="media/FLVSampleVideo.ogv">
  </video>
  <video controls height="150" width="200" src="media/WMESampleVideo.ogg">
  </video>
  <video controls height="150" width="200" src="media/FLVSampleVideo.ogg">
  </video>
</article>
</section>
</body>
</html>
```

```
<video controls height="150" width="200" src="media/FLVSampleVideo.ogv">
 </video>
```

The above snippet is that of an html 5 video tag which can be used to render Ogg (Theora) video. The above tag is going to render the FLVSampleVideo.ogv file into a canvas of 200x150 pixels size along with video controls. We are rendering 3 videos one each from the processing methods we used to encode them. Opening the page in various browsers renders them as follows...

Video

Figure 68 - Video Renders Perfectly in Chrome

Video

Figure 69 - Silent Rendering Errors in Firefox

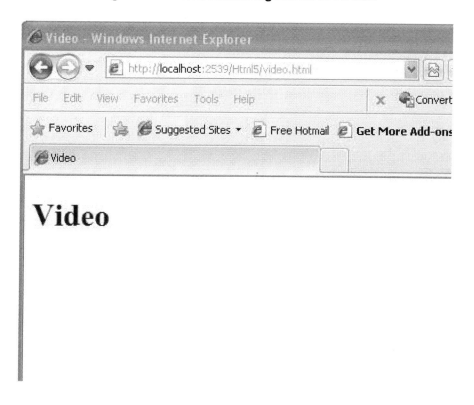

Figure 70 - Video Not Rendered in IE 8

Video

Figure 71 - Video Rendered Perfectly in Opera

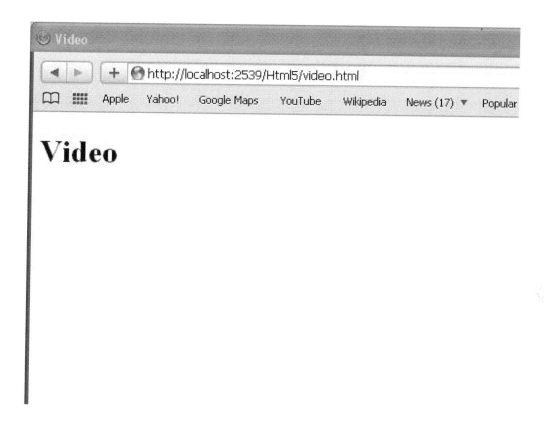

Figure 72 - Video Not Rendered in Safari

Creating the Audio page

Create an audio page audio.html using notepad with the following contents. We are using two freely available mp3 and ogg (vorbis) files on the internet for the tutorial.

```
audio.html code

<!DOCTYPE html>

<html>
<head>
<meta charset="utf-8">
<title>Audio</title>
</head>
<body>
<section id="wrapper">
  <header>
    <h1>Audio</h1>
```

```
      </header>
<article>
    <audio controls src="http://www.a1sounddownload.com/freesounds5/7soundsamples2010.mp3">
    </audio>
    <audio controls src="http://www.vorbis.com/music/Epoq-Lepidoptera.ogg">
    </audio>
</article>
</section>
</body>
</html>
```

You can encode vorbis files from other audio formats using similar methods shown earlier in this chapter.

Let's open the audio.html page in various browsers and check if it works.

Audio

Figure 73 - Chrome Play Audio Perfectly

Audio

Figure 74 - Firefox Only Plays Vorbis

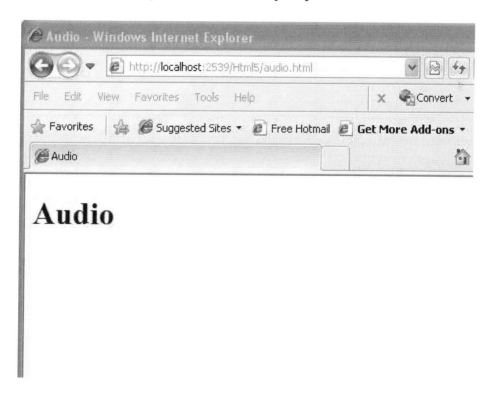

Figure 75 - IE Doesn't Play Any Audio

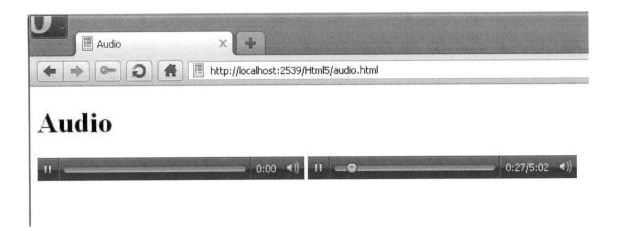

Figure 76 - Opera Only Plays Vorbis

Figure 77 - Safari Doesn't Play Anything

A Quick Walkthrough of the Specifications

The video tag has the following attributes

src

poster

preload

autoplay

loop

controls

width

height

If the poster attribute is set the image specified is shown when the video is not available.

The audio tag has the following attributes

src

preload

autoplay

loop

controls

Audio & Video tags can have multiple source elements inside them if the src attribute is not used. It has the following attributes

src

type

media

The type attribute is used to judge whether the video/audio can be played in the browser, it could include codecs required also. The Browser chooses which of the following source elements is fit for playback in the browser. Multiple source tags give browser the option of choosing from multiple formats the one which it can play.

```
<video controls>
  <source src="foo.ogg" type="video/ogg">
  <source src="foo.mp4">
  Your browser does not support the <code>video</code> element. This is the fallback content.
</video>
```

The video/audio tag can also have fallback content which will get displayed on older browsers also we can put a flash player for use on older browsers in the fallback content. E.g. below if the ogg video cannot be played in older browsers the cortado java applet is used to play the ogg video

```
<video src="my_ogg_video.ogg" controls width="320" height="240">
  <object type="application/x-java-applet"
      width="320" height="240">
    <param name="archive" value="cortado.jar">
    <param name="code" value="com.fluendo.player.Cortado.class">
    <param name="url" value="my_ogg_video.ogg">
    <p>You need to install Java to play this file.</p>
  </object>
</video>
```

Various events are raised when handling media e.g. abort, canplay, canplaythrough, canshowcurrentframe, dataunavailable, durationchange, emptied, empty, ended, error, laodedfirsttime, loadedmetadata, loadstart, pause, play, progress, ratechange, seeked, seeking, suspend, timeupdate, volumechange, waiting etc.

Retrospective

We used Firefogg plugin and FFMpeg to encode videos into Ogg (Theora). They can be used similarly to encode audios into Ogg (Vorbis) which is left to the reader to try out. We tried simple Audio and Video playback in various browsers with mixed results.

Chapter 9- GeoLocation

In this chapter we are going to have a look at the HTML 5 Geolocation API. This API can be used to serve location specific content to the user easily. Till now browser applications were using IP address for geo location which is not very reliable in the case of mobile devices. The HTML 5 geo location api when used in a geo location aware browser like the latest version of firefox will hook onto the GPS device on the system (usually mobiles) which if not found will fallback to IP Address based geo location detection.

We are going to build a small application using JQuery, GeoLocation API and the Google Map API to detect the Geo Location of the user and then will mark the location on a Google Map. Soon all mobile browsers are going to support location aware applications.

We assume you have all the 5 top browsers installed on your desktop. Let's get started with Google Map signup for the API at http://code.google.com/apis/maps/signup.html

You have to provide the domain name for your web application. Click Generate API Key button and signin with your google login id. Your API Key will show up on the next screen. Note it down and we will use it in our development. There is no limit on the number of requests you can make in a day and there are no charges either.

Sign Up for the Google Maps API

The Google Maps API lets you embed Google Maps in your own web pages. A single Maps API key is valid for a single "directory" or domain. See this FAQ for more information. You must have a Google Account to get a Maps API key, and your API key will be connected to your Google Account.

Here are some highlights from the terms for those of you who aren't lawyers:

- **There is no limit on the number of page views you may generate per day using the Maps API.** See this FAQ for more information.
- **There is a limit on the number of geocode requests per day.** See this FAQ for more information.
- **The Maps API does not include advertising.** If we ever decide to change this policy, we will give you at least 90 days notice via the announcements lists.
- If you use other APIs in conjunction with the Maps API, you should also review the terms for the other APIs. Note in particular that the GoogleBar in the JS Maps API uses the AJAX Search API, and that API has its own terms.
- **Your service must be freely accessible to end users.** To use Google mapping technology in other types of applications, please use Google Maps API Premier. See this FAQ for more information.
- **You may not alter or obscure the logos or attribution on the map.**
- You must indicate whether your application is using a sensor (such as a GPS locator) to determine the user's location.
- You may use the API (except for the Static Maps API) in websites or in software applications. For websites, please sign up with the URL where your implementation can be found. For other software applications, please sign up with the URL of the page where your application can be downloaded.
- Google will upgrade the APIs periodically. To be notified of updates, please subscribe to the announcements lists.
- Remember that we reserve the right to suspend or terminate your use of the service at any time, so please read through the FAQ and forum posts to decide whether your site meets the Terms of Use before you begin API integration.

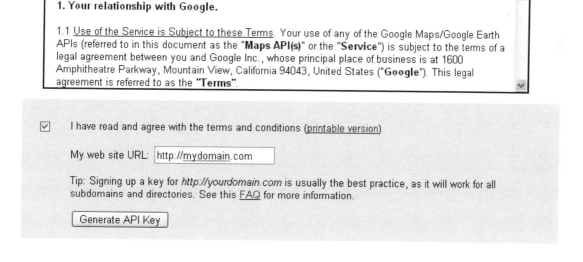

Last updated: November 26, 2008

1. Your relationship with Google.

1.1 Use of the Service is Subject to these Terms. Your use of any of the Google Maps/Google Earth APIs (referred to in this document as the "**Maps API(s)**" or the "**Service**") is subject to the terms of a legal agreement between you and Google Inc., whose principal place of business is at 1600 Amphitheatre Parkway, Mountain View, California 94043, United States ("**Google**"). This legal agreement is referred to as the "**Terms**".

☑   I have read and agree with the terms and conditions (printable version)

My web site URL: http://mydomain.com

Tip: Signing up a key for *http://yourdomain.com* is usually the best practice, as it will work for all subdomains and directories. See this FAQ for more information.

[Generate API Key]

Figure 78 - Google Maps API Signup

Sign Up for the Google Maps API

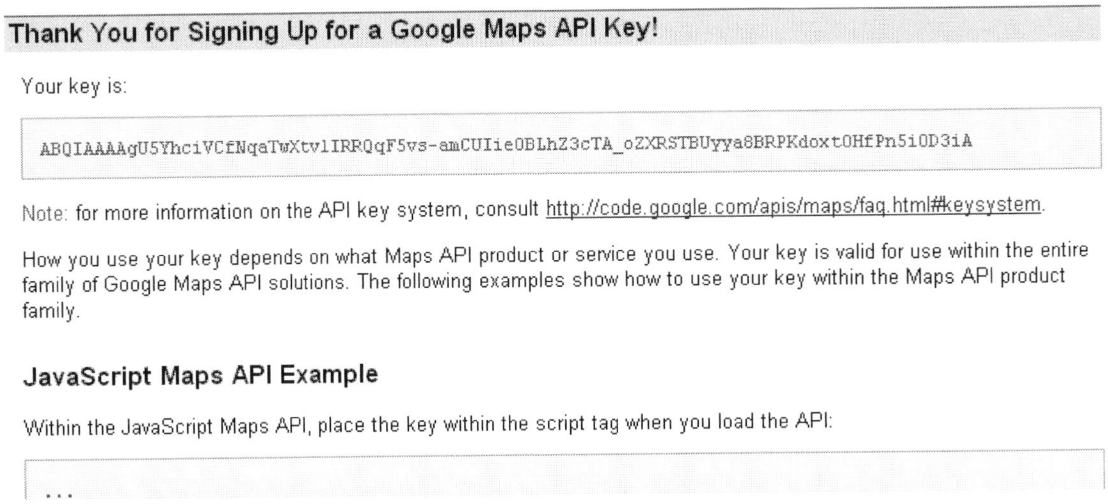

Thank You for Signing Up for a Google Maps API Key!

Your key is:

ABQIAAAAgU5YhciVCfNqaTwXtvlIRRQqF5vs-amCUIieOBLhZ3cTA_oZXRSTBUyya8BRPKdoxtOHfPn5iOD3iA

Note: for more information on the API key system, consult http://code.google.com/apis/maps/faq.html#keysystem.

How you use your key depends on what Maps API product or service you use. Your key is valid for use within the entire family of Google Maps API solutions. The following examples show how to use your key within the Maps API product family.

JavaScript Maps API Example

Within the JavaScript Maps API, place the key within the script tag when you load the API:

...

Figure 79 - Google Map API Key

We will be using the JQuery API which is included in the source code bundle accompanying this book. Create an html page with the name geolocation.html, using notepad or any other editor or in a Visual Studio web application project, with the following contents.

Geolocation.html code

```
<!DOCTYPE html>

<html>
<head>
    <title>GeoLocation</title>
    <script type="text/javascript" charset="utf-8" src="js/jquery-
1.3.2.js"></script>
    <script src="http://maps.google.com/maps?file=api&amp;v=2&amp;sensor=true

&amp;key=ABQIAAAAgU5YhciVCfNqaTwXtvlIRRSQKSwulhIHnqFqOm2ZluuckFsjVxRLZ8zEq3X-
4T5tiPoW1HQcuqLffg" type="text/javascript">
    </script>

    <script type="text/javascript">
        var themap;
        var long;
```

```
            var lat;
            var thepoint;
            var themarker;

                $(window).unload(GUnload);

        $(document).ready(function() {
            themap = new GMap2(document.getElementById("map_canvas"));
            themap.setCenter(new GLatLng(12.971606, 77.594376), 14);
                    themap.setUIToDefault();

            if (navigator.geolocation) {
                navigator.geolocation.getCurrentPosition(function(position) {
                    lat = position.coords.latitude;
                    long = position.coords.longitude;
                    $('#longitude').html(long);
                    $('#latitude').html(lat);

                    themap.clearOverlays();
                    thepoint = new GLatLng(lat, long);
                    themarker = new GMarker(thepoint);
                    themap.setCenter(thepoint, 14);
                    themap.addOverlay(themarker);
                });
            } else {
                alert("geolocation services are not supported by your
browser/device.");
            }
        });
    </script>
</head>
<body>

Longitude<br />
<div id="longitude">???</div>
Latitude<br />
<div id="latitude">???</div>
<br /><br />
<div id="map_canvas" style="width: 800px; height: 600px"></div>

</body>
</html>
```

This is all the code required for a basic geo location based map application. In a real application the geolocation data should be put into a hidden form field in the login page and sent to the server so that the rest of the application can serve location aware services.

Let's go through the code.

```
<script type="text/javascript" charset="utf-8" src="js/jquery-1.3.2.js"></script>
```

This line includes the JQuery javascript library on the page for our use. It has to be kept in the 'js' folder. If you have a different version of the JQuery library make sure the file name on the filesystem matches with the file name in this statement.

```
<script src="http://maps.google.com/maps?file=api&amp;v=2&amp;sensor=true
&amp;key=ABQIAAAAgU5YhciVCfNqaTwXtvlIRRSQKSwulhIHnqFqOm2ZluuckFsjVxRLZ8zEq3X-
4T5tiPoW1HQcuqLffg" type="text/javascript">
</script>
```

This line loads the Google Maps javascript library. Note that we say 'sensor=true' which is an indication to google that our program will use sensors. Don't really know how that is needed by the API. The other thing to note is 'key=ABQIAAAAgU5YhciVCfNqaTwXtvlIRRSQKSwulhIHnqFqOm2ZluuckFsjVxR LZ8zEq3X-4T5tiPoW1HQcuqLffg' this is our Google Maps API Key. You should use your key instead especially in a production application.

The next script tag is the portion which contains our application functionality. But before we look at that lets see the code we have put in the body of the html page.

```
Longitude<br />
<div id="longitude">???</div>
Latitude<br />
<div id="latitude">???</div>
<br /><br />
<div id="map_canvas" style="width: 800px; height: 600px"></div>
```

We have created two divs one each for displaying the longitude and latitude. Followed by a div to display the map named 'map_canvas'. The longitude and latitude have a fallback content of '???' which gets displayed if the browser is not geolocation aware. The map canvas is empty and of 800x600 pixels in size, which we could set to anything.

```
var themap;
var long;
var lat;
var thepoint;
var themarker;
```

The above variables store the map, longitude, latitude, point object and the marker object.

```
$(window).unload(GUnload);
```

The above statement hooks the GUnload function to the window unload event. Which is a google api specific function.

```
$(document).ready(function() {
        themap = new GMap2(document.getElementById("map_canvas"));
        themap.setCenter(new GLatLng(12.971606, 77.594376), 14);
            themap.setUIToDefault();

        if (navigator.geolocation) {
            navigator.geolocation.getCurrentPosition(function(position) {
                lat = position.coords.latitude;
                long = position.coords.longitude;
                $('#longitude').html(long);
                $('#latitude').html(lat);

                themap.clearOverlays();
                thepoint = new GLatLng(lat, long);
                themarker = new GMarker(thepoint);
                themap.setCenter(thepoint, 14);
                themap.addOverlay(themarker);
            });
        } else {
            alert("geolocation services are not supported by your
browser/device.");
        }
    });
```

This is the meat of our application. We use the $(document).ready(…) to execute our code when the browser has done loading the full dom of the web page and is ready.

We Initialise the GMap2 object by passing it the div element where our map should be displayed. Then we center the map to an arbitrary location. We use '14' as a parameter along with it which implies the zoom level of the map. And then we set the map UI to default.

We use an if-then-else statement to check if the browser is location aware or not. If not we display an appropriate alert, if it is we execute the rest of the code. We call the arynchronous method 'navigator.geolocation.getCurrentPosition(…)' which calls back our function with the position parameter. We extract the latitude and longitude values into our variables. And next we display the values in their respective divs using '$('#<div id>').html(<HTML Content to Set>);

We clear all overlays. And create a GLatLong object which is basically a container to hold longitude and latitude and then it is used by the rest of the Google Maps API. We create a marker object and we set the center of the map to the detected Geo Location and set the zoom level to 14. And then we add the marker as an overlay.

Open the page in Firefox. The browser requests for our permission to use the geo location services on the computer.

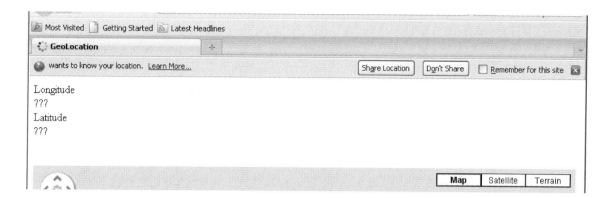

Figure 80 - Geo Location Request Prompt in Firefox

Till we permit the browser to access the underlying GPS device the Geo Location functionality won't work, and the longitude and latitude divs show the fallback text of '???'. After we permit the browser the page renders a map centered at our detected geo location with zoom level of 14.

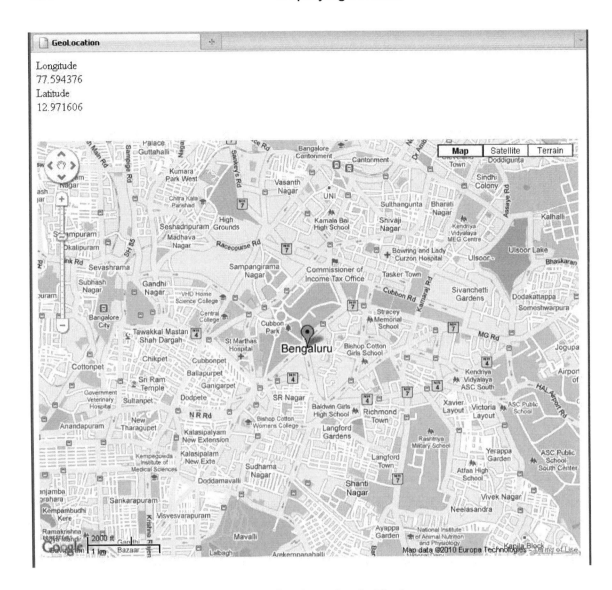

Figure 81 - Geo Location in Firefox

We can use GeoLocator 1.0.1 addon for Firefox to test out location aware applications. The addon allows us to set the geo location for the browser to any arbitrary Longitude and Latitude enabling the QA to test the application under various scenarios. Let's take the addon for a spin. Download it from https://addons.mozilla.org/en-US/firefox/addon/14046

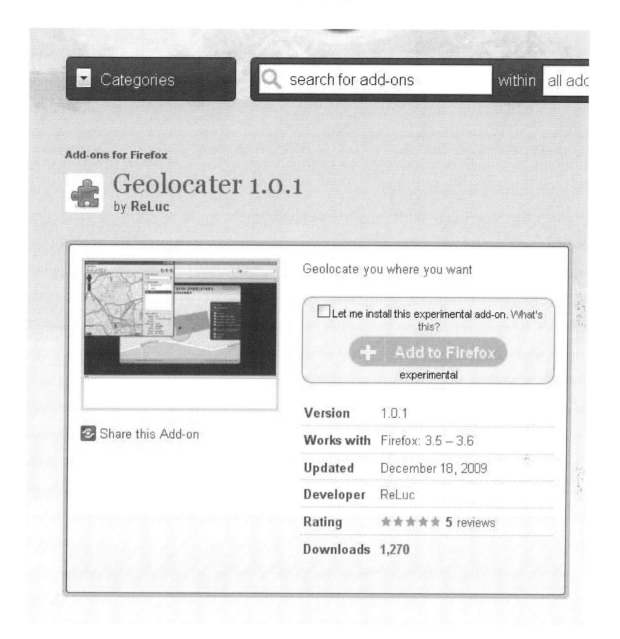

Figure 82 - GeoLocator Addon For Firefox

After installation restart firefox and click Tools->GeoLocator->Manage, Click GeoLocations->New enter 'Manhattan, NYC'

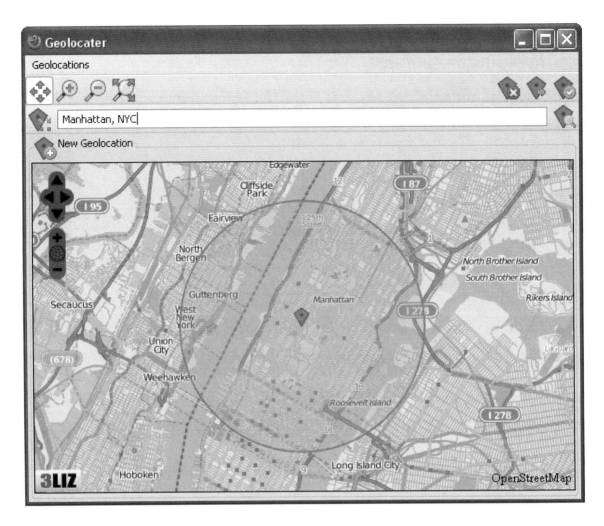

Figure 83 - Set GeoLocation to Manhattan, NYC

Click the button 'Switch from search to select geolocation' and click Geolocations->Save. See below.

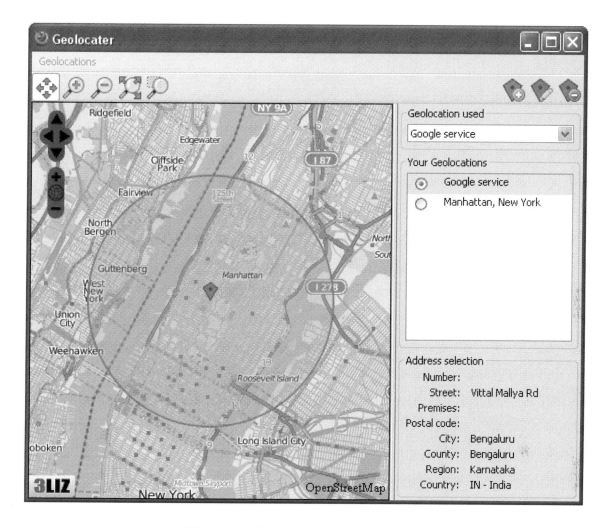

Figure 84 - Save the new GeoLocation

Let's open the GeoLocation.html again in firefox. This time it prompts us for permission and also asks us for the geolocation to use. Selecting 'Google Service' will use the IP Address based geolocation resolution and selecting 'Manhattan, New York' will use the Manhattan GeoLocation. Let's choose Manhattan and click 'Share Location'. See below.

Figure 85 - Selecting Manhattan

The page then renders as shown below.

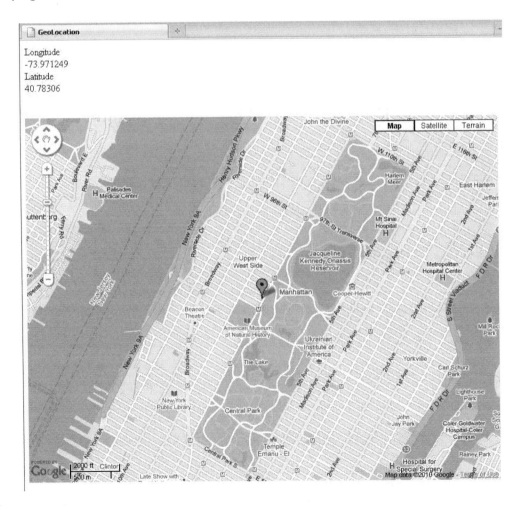

Figure 86 - Manhattan on the Map

Let's try the same application with IE, Chrome, Opera and Safari.

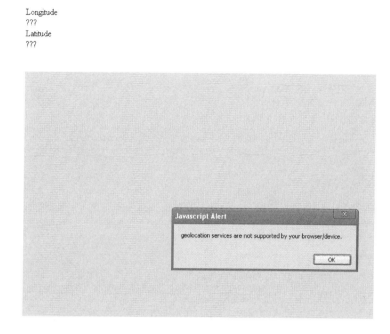

Figure 87 – No GeoLocation Support in Chrome

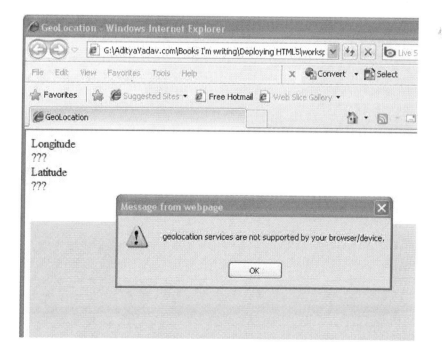

Figure 88 - No GeoLocation Support in IE

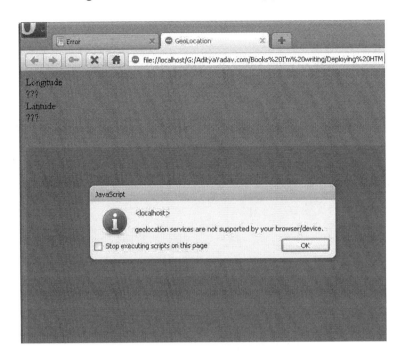

Figure 89 - No GeoLocation Support in Opera

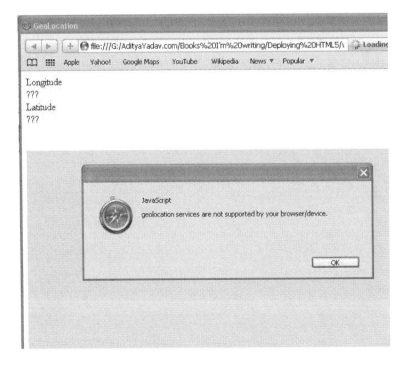

Figure 90 - No GeoLocation Support in Safari

A Quick Walkthrough of the Specifications

An example of an oneshot position request

```
function showMap(position) {
    // Show a map centered at (position.coords.latitude, position.coords.longitude).
}


// One-shot position request.
navigator.geolocation.getCurrentPosition(showMap);
```

An example of a request to continuously monitor the geo location with error handling.

```
function scrollMap(position) {
  // Scrolls the map so that it is centered at (position.coords.latitude, position.coords.longitude).
}


function handleError(error) {
  // Update a div element with error.message.
}


// Request repeated updates.
var watchId = navigator.geolocation.watchPosition(scrollMap, handleError);


function buttonClickHandler() {
  // Cancel the updates when the user clicks a button.
  navigator.geolocation.clearWatch(watchId);
}
```

Requesting for the position which is not older than 10 minutes or 600000 ms old.

```
navigator.geolocation.getCurrentPosition(successCallback,
                      errorCallback,
                      {maximumAge:600000});
```

Retrospective

In this chapter we saw how to use the HTML 5 GeoLocation API. And we used a firefox addon to set our geo location to Manhattan, NYC for testing purposes. We saw that the webpage doesn't work in the other 4 browsers. And then we went through an explanation of the GeoLocation API Specification.

Chapter 10- Web Storage

In this chapter we are going to check out web storage features of HTML 5. These are namely sessionStorage and localStorage. Let's dive quickly into the example straightaway by creating an html file 'webstorage.html' with the following contents.

webstorage.html Code

```html
<!DOCTYPE html>
<!-- some browsers support globalStorage also. we will not be covering that-->
<html>
<head>
<meta http-equiv="Content-Type" content="text/html; charset=ISO-8859-1">
<title>Web Storage: Session & Local</title>
<script type="text/javascript" charset="utf-8" src="js/jquery-1.3.2.js"></script>
<script type="text/javascript">
  function storeInSession() {
    sessionStorage.setItem("Name", $("#Name").val());
  }

  function retrieveFromSession() {
    $("#Name").val(sessionStorage.getItem("Name"));
  }

  function clearSession() {
    sessionStorage.removeItem("Name");
    $("#Name").val('');
  }

  function storeInLocal() {
    localStorage.setItem("Email", $("#Email").val());
  }

  function retrieveFromLocal() {
    $("#Email").val(localStorage.getItem("Email"));
  }

  function clearLocal() {
    localStorage.removeItem("Email");
    $("#Email").val('');
  }

</script>
</head>
<body>
<h1>Web Storage: Session & Local</h1>
<h2>Session Storage</h2>
```

```
Name <input id="Name" type="text" placeholder="Enter Your Name" /><br />
<input type="button" value="Store" onclick="storeInSession();" /><input type="button"
value="Retrieve" onclick="retrieveFromSession();" /><input type="button" value="Clear"
onclick="clearSession();" /><br />

<h2>Local Storage</h2>
Email <input id="Email" type="text" placeholder="Enter Your Email" /><br />
<input type="button" value="Store" onclick="storeInLocal();" /><input type="button"
value="Retrieve" onclick="retrieveFromLocal();" /><input type="button" value="Clear"
onclick="clearLocal();" /><br />
</body>
</html>
```

```
Name <input id="Name" type="text" placeholder="Enter Your Name" /><br />
```

The above line renders the text 'Name' and an input text box with the id 'Name' and placeholder 'Enter Your Name'

```
<input type="button" value="Store" onclick="storeInSession();" /><input type="button" value="Retrieve" onclick="retrieveFromSession();" /><input type="button" value="Clear" onclick="clearSession();" /><br />
```

The above code renders 3 buttons one each for Store, Retrieve and Clear. When clicked they call 'storeInSession', 'retreiveFromSession' and 'clearSession' respectively.

```
Email <input id="Email" type="text" placeholder="Enter Your Email" /><br />
```

The above code renders the text 'Email' and an input text box with the id 'Email' and placeholder 'Enter Your Email'.

```
<input type="button" value="Store" onclick="storeInLocal();" /><input type="button" value="Retrieve" onclick="retrieveFromLocal();" /><input type="button" value="Clear" onclick="clearLocal();" /><br />
```

The above code renders 3 buttons one each for Store, Retrieve and Clear. When clicked they call 'storeInLocal' , 'retrieveFromLocal' and 'clearLocal' respectively.

Let's look at the javascript code that powers the page.

```
function storeInSession() {
    sessionStorage.setItem("Name", $("#Name").val());
}
```

The above method sets an item 'Name' in sessionStorage with the value entered by the user in the 'Name' text box.

```
function retrieveFromSession() {
    $("#Name").val(sessionStorage.getItem("Name"));
}
```

The above code retrieves the value for the key 'Name' from the sessionStorage and sets it as the value of the text box with the id 'Name'

```
function clearSession() {
    sessionStorage.removeItem("Name");
    $("#Name").val('');
}
```

The above code removes the item from the sessionStorage with the key 'Name'. And clears the text box with the id 'Name'

```
function storeInLocal() {
    localStorage.setItem("Email", $("#Email").val());
}
```

The above code stores the value entered by the user in the textbox with the id 'Email', into localStorage with the key 'Email'

```
function retrieveFromLocal() {
    $("#Email").val(localStorage.getItem("Email"));
}
```

The above code retrieves the value from localStorage with the key 'Email'. And sets it as the value of the text box with the id 'Email'

```
function clearLocal() {
    localStorage.removeItem("Email");
    $("#Email").val('');
}
```

The above code clears the value from the localStorage which has the key 'Email' and it also clears the text box with the 'Email' id.

Let's take it for a spin. We will enter 'MyName' and 'MyEmail' in the two text boxes and click store for both of them. Then we will delete the content in both the text boxes and click Retrieve for both of them. Let's try it out in all the browsers.

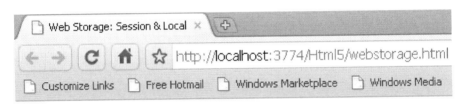

Web Storage: Session & Local

Session Storage

Name [Enter Your Name]
[Store] [Retrieve] [Clear]

Local Storage

Email [MyEmail]
[Store] [Retrieve] [Clear]

Figure 91 - Only Local Storage Works in Chrome

Web Storage: Session & Local

Session Storage

Local Storage

Figure 92 - Both Session & Local Storage Work in Firefox

Figure 93 - Both Local & Session Storage Don't Work in IE

Web Storage: Session & Local

Session Storage

Name [   ]
[Store] [Retrieve] [Clear]

Local Storage

Email [   ]
[Store] [Retrieve] [Clear]

Figure 94 - Both Session & Local Storage Don't Work in Opera

Figure 95 - Both Session & Local Storage Works in Safari

A Quick Walkthrough of the Specifications

The sessionStorage is accessible to any page opened from the same site. localStorage lasts beyond the current session.

length - returns the number of key/value pairs currently present in the list associated with the object.

key(n) - method returns the name of the nth key in the list.

getItem(key) - method returns the current value associated with the given key

setItem(key, value) - method must store the value and associate it with the key provided

removeItem(key) - method causes the key/value pair with the given key to be removed

clear() - method atomically causes all key/value pairs to be removed

The 'storage' event fires when the storage area changes.

The key attribute represents the key being changed.

The oldValue attribute represents the old value of the key being changed.

The newValue attribute represents the new value of the key being changed.

The url attribute represents the address of the document whose key changed.

The storageArea attribute represents the Storage object that was affected.

Retrospective

In this chapter we saw a small example of local and session storage, some browsers provide globalStorage too which we have not covered as we are not sure if it will become a part of the specification or not.

Chapter 11- Server Sent Events

In the pre-HTML5 era we as developers used a lot of non standard means like Pushlets, Repeated Ajax Polls etc. These methods caused unreasonable strain on the browser and the server. HTML 5 standardizes a server streaming event pushing mechanism aka Server Sent Events. We are going to build one example and test it.

We will need Visual Studio for this exercise even though the concept is applicable to any server back end language or tooling as long as it can keep a connection open and flush events to the HTTP stream. Anything would do Java, PHP, Python etc. But for the purpose of this exercise we will use ASP.Net HTTP Handlers for the backend while the front end will be a simple html page.

Let's create a file pushevents.html in Visual Studio as follows.

pushevents.html Code

```
<!DOCTYPE html>
<!-- Feature Tested in Opera 10.10 beta doesn't work in versions after that
    The Server Sent Events Specifications has changed and Opera is abandoning what they have
implemented so far
    But this should give you an idea of what this feature will be like.
    -->

<html>
<head>
<meta http-equiv="Content-Type" content="text/html; charset=ISO-8859-1">
<title>Push Events: Stock Chart</title>
    <script type="text/javascript" charset="utf-8" src="js/jquery-1.3.2.js"></script>
    <script type="text/javascript" charset="utf-8" src="js/RGraph.common.js"></script>
    <script type="text/javascript" charset="utf-8" src="js/RGraph.line.js"></script>

    <script type="text/javascript">
      var stockData = new Array();

    function addToStockData(event) {
      var data = event.data.split("\n");
      var quote = data[0];

      $("#messages").html($("#messages").html() + quote + "<br/>");
```

```
            stockData.push(quote);
            if (stockData.length >= 100) stockData.shift();

            redrawGraph();
        }

        function redrawGraph() {
            var line = new RGraph.Line("graph", stockData);
            line.Set('chart.background.barcolor1', 'rgba(255,255,255,1)');
            line.Set('chart.background.barcolor2', 'rgba(255,255,255,1)');
            line.Set('chart.background.grid.color', 'rgba(238,238,238,1)');
            line.Set('chart.colors', ['rgba(255,0,0,1)']);
            line.Set('chart.linewidth', 2);
            line.Set('chart.filled', false);
            line.Set('chart.hmargin', 5);
            line.Set('chart.gutter', 40);
            line.Draw();

        }

        $(document).ready(function () {
            document.getElementsByTagName("event-source")[0].addEventListener("newstockquote",
addToStockData, false);
        });

    </script>
</head>
<body>
    <event-source id="stock" src="PushEvents.ashx"></event-source>
    <h1>Live Stock Chart</h1>
    <div>
        <canvas id="graph" width="475" height="250">[Please wait...]</canvas>
    </div>
    <div id="messages" style="height: 400; width: 400;"></div>
</body>
</html>
```

```
<script type="text/javascript" charset="utf-8" src="js/RGraph.common.js"></script>
<script type="text/javascript" charset="utf-8" src="js/RGraph.line.js"></script>
```

The two above javascript statements include the RGraph libraries. RGraph is used to draw graphs on HTML 5 Canvas. We include the common RGraph library in the first statement and then in the second statement we include the RGraph library for drawing line graphs. Every graph type requires its own RGraph javascript file along with the common RGraph javascript file.

```
var stockData = new Array();
```

This statement creates a dynamic Array to store the Stock Quotes.

```
function addToStockData(event) {
    var data = event.data.split("\n");
    var quote = data[0];

    $("#messages").html($("#messages").html() + quote + "<br/>");

    stockData.push(quote);
    if (stockData.length >= 100) stockData.shift();

    redrawGraph();
}
```

This function takes an event object and splits it using a newline character as a delimiter and takes the first token as the stockquote. It appends the stock quote to the 'messages' div. It then pushes the quote to the end of the stockData array. If the length of the array is greater than or equal to 100 it removes one quote from the front of the array and shifts the other entire quotes one place to fill in the gap. This is done so that we draw a graph of only upto last 100 stock quotes. It then calls the redraw graph function.

```
function redrawGraph() {
    var line = new RGraph.Line("graph", stockData);
    line.Set('chart.background.barcolor1', 'rgba(255,255,255,1)');
    line.Set('chart.background.barcolor2', 'rgba(255,255,255,1)');
    line.Set('chart.background.grid.color', 'rgba(238,238,238,1)');
    line.Set('chart.colors', ['rgba(255,0,0,1)']);
    line.Set('chart.linewidth', 2);
    line.Set('chart.filled', false);
    line.Set('chart.hmargin', 5);
    line.Set('chart.gutter', 40);
    line.Draw();

}
```

The redraw function creates a line graph object and links it to the Canvas with the id as 'graph' and passes it the stock quote data. It sets the various properties and then draws the graph on the canvas.

```
$(document).ready(function () {
    document.getElementsByTagName("event-source")[0].addEventListener("newstockquote",
addToStockData, false);
});
```

The above code calls the inline function when the document is ready. The inline function gets the first event source tag and adds an event listener to it which calls the addToStockData function we saw earlier. The event name is 'newstockquote' which is the same as the event code being delivered to the page via the server sent event stream. (One stream can have many event codes to minimize connection usage).

PushEvents.ashx Code

```csharp
<%@ WebHandler Language="C#" Class="PushEvents" %>

using System;
using System.Web;
using System.Threading;

public class PushEvents : IHttpHandler {

    public void ProcessRequest (HttpContext context) {
        context.Response.Buffer = false;
        context.Response.BufferOutput = false;
        context.Response.ContentType = "application/x-dom-event-stream";

        Random random = new Random();
        int stockPrice = random.Next(0, 100);

        while (true)
        {
            int incr = random.Next(0, 6) - 3;
            stockPrice += incr;
            if (stockPrice > 100) stockPrice = 100;
            if (stockPrice < 0) stockPrice = 0;

            context.Response.Output.Write("Event: newstockquote\n");
            context.Response.Output.Write("data: " + stockPrice.ToString() +
"\n\n");
            context.Response.Output.Flush();
            context.Response.Flush();
            Thread.Sleep(1000); // one second delay in between sending events
        }
```

```
    }

    public bool IsReusable {
        get {
            return false;
        }
    }
}
```

The HTTP Handler is contained in one method 'ProcessRequest'.

```
context.Response.Buffer = false;
context.Response.BufferOutput = false;
```

The two statements turn off buffering. We want to be able to send real-time events to the browser.

```
context.Response.ContentType = "application/x-dom-event-stream";
```

The above statement sets the content type of the response to 'application/x-dom-event-stream' which is mandatory content type for Server Side Event Streams.

```
        Random random = new Random();
        int stockPrice = random.Next(0, 100);
```

These statements initialize a random number generator and set the initial stock price.

```
        while (true)
        {
            .
            .
            .
        }
```

The while loop is used to generate a continous stream of stock prices.

```
int incr = random.Next(0, 6) - 3;
stockPrice += incr;
```

The above statements calculate a random variation between -3 to +3 and then apply it to the last stock price.

```
if (stockPrice > 100) stockPrice = 100;
if (stockPrice < 0) stockPrice = 0;
```

The stock price has to be in between 0 and 100 these two checks make sure that the 0-100 limit is not crossed.

```
context.Response.Output.Write("Event: newstockquote\n");
context.Response.Output.Write("data: " + stockPrice.ToString() + "\n\n");
```

The first statement writes the event name to the stream as 'Event: <eventname>\n' this statement has to end with a newline character, carriage returns and other characters are not valid. The second statement delivers the payload as 'data: <payload>\n\n' followed by one newline character to end the payload and another one to end the event.

```
context.Response.Output.Flush();
context.Response.Flush();
```

These two statements flush the event to the browser without buffering it.

```
Thread.Sleep(1000);
```

The last statement cause a 1 second delay between two consecutive events in the event stream.

When you run the pushevents.html page in Opera 10.10 beta it renders a realtime stock graph as shown below. With the payload of each event listed in te div below.

Live Stock Chart

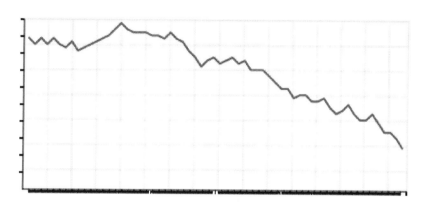

49
47
49
47
49
47
46
48
45
46
47
48
49

Figure 96 - Opera 10.10beta Supports Server Sent Events

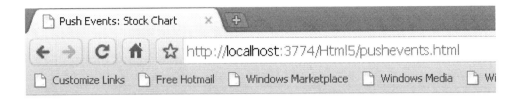

Live Stock Chart

Figure 97 - Chrome Doesn't Support Server Sent Events

Live Stock Chart

Figure 98 - Firefox Doesn't Support Server Sent Events

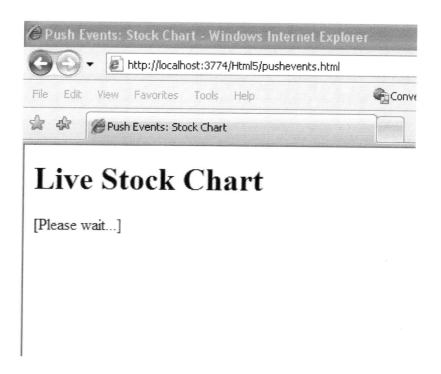

Figure 99 - IE Doesn't Support Server Sent Events

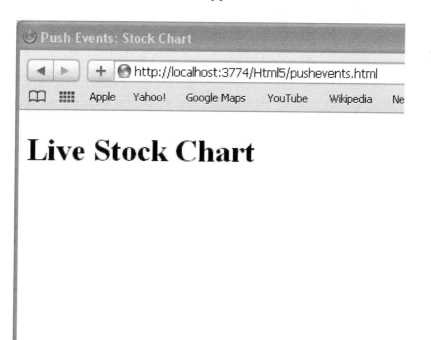

Figure 100 - Safari Doesn't Support Server Sent Events

A Quick Walkthrough of the Specifications

You will find that the specifications are different from what Opera has implemented. And that's the reason Opera has taken away the implementation from the latest build of its browser.

To enable servers to push events to the browser over HTTP the specification specifies the EventSource object.

```
var source = new EventSource('updates.cgi');

source.onmessage = function (event) {
  alert(event.data);
};
```

On the server side the 'updates.cgi' script sends events in a stream in the following format. It should use the 'text/event-stream' mime type.

```
data: This is the first message.

data: This is the second message, it
data: has two lines.

data: This is the third message.
```

A blank line denotes the end of the event. Each event can contain multiple lines starting with 'data:'. All of the content in an event will be delivered with '\n' seperators in one text string retrievable from 'event.data'

The EventSource has onopen, onmessage and onerror events which can be used. It also has a close() method to close the eventsource connection.

It has a readyState attribute which can have CONNECTION, OPEN or CLOSED values.

```
: test stream

data: first event
id: 1
```

The Event can also contain an id starting with 'id:' this can be recovered from the lastEventId attribute of the EventSource. Any line starting with a ':' is a comment line and is usually sent by the server code to prevent disconnection, every 15 seconds or so, due to the way legacy http proxy servers function.

Retrospective

In this chapter we used an older build of Opera browser to try out the Server Side Event functionality. This has been taken off the latest build of Opera as the specifications have changed. And as of now none of the browsers implement the correct specification. The reader should try out SSE with the correct specs when browsers implement it. The current example should not be used for production code.

Chapter 12- Workers

HTML 5 provides the possibility of background threads to exist which are native OS threads and can be used for asynchronous computation intensive operations. We will be building a web worker to calculate prime numbers below the given maximum number.

Let's start by creating an html file called webworker.html with the following contents.

webworker.html Code

```html
<!DOCTYPE html>

<html>
<head>
  <title>WebWorker: Prime Finder</title>
  <script type="text/javascript" charset="utf-8" src="js/jquery-1.3.2.js"></script>
  <script type="text/javascript" charset="utf-8" src="js/json2.js"></script>


  <script type="text/javascript">
    var worker;
    $(document).ready(function () {
      worker = new Worker('js/prime-finder-web-worker.js');
      // Watch for messages from the worker
      worker.onmessage = function (event) {
        var data = event.data;
        $("#message").html(data);
        $('#primestable tr:last').after(data);
      };

      worker.onerror = function (error) {
        $("#error").html(error.message);
        throw error;
      };
    });

    function findprimes() {
      $("#primestable tr:gt(0)").remove();
      var maximum = $("#maximum").val();
      worker.postMessage(maximum);
    };
  </script>
</head>
<body>
```

```
<div style="width:400px; border:dotted blue;background: white">
  <b>Maximum</b> <input id="maximum" value="20" /><input type="button" value="Find Primes..."
onclick="findprimes();" /><br />
  <table id="primestable">
    <tr>
      <th>Primes</th>
    </tr>
  </table>
</div>
<b>Last Message From Worker</b><br />
<div id="message" style="width:400px; height:50px; border:dotted blue;background:
white"></div><br />

<b>Last Worker Error</b><br />
<div id="error" style="width:400px; height:50px; border:dotted blue;background: white"></div><br
/>


</body>
</html>
```

```
<script type="text/javascript" charset="utf-8" src="js/jquery-1.3.2.js"></script>
<script type="text/javascript" charset="utf-8" src="js/json2.js"></script>
```

These two javascript statements include the JQuery and Json libraries in the html
page.

```
var worker;
```

This variable stores the reference to the worker. We are going to create one
worker in this example but we can have as many as limited by the resources on
the OS.

```
$(document).ready(function () {
    worker = new Worker('js/prime-finder-web-worker.js');
    // Watch for messages from the worker
    worker.onmessage = function (event) {
        var data = event.data;
        $("#message").html(data);
        $('#primestable tr:last').after(data);
    };

    worker.onerror = function (error) {
        $("#error").html(error.message);
```

```
        throw error;
    };
});
```

This method hooks the inline function to be executed when the document is ready. The inline function creates a worker from the 'prime-finder-web-worker.js' javascript file.

Next it hooks a function as the workers onmessage event handler. The event handler function retrieves the string data which the worker has sent and adds it to the 'message' div as contents, so we can see whats the last message from the worker, just for debugging purposes.

The inline function also hooks a function as the event handler for the workers 'onerror' event

```
function findprimes() {
    $("#primestable tr:gt(0)").remove();
    var maximum = $("#maximum").val();
    worker.postMessage(maximum);
};
```

This method removes all the previous found prime number entries from the 'primestable' recovers the maximum value from the 'maximum' text box. And then posts a message to the worker with the maximum value as the message content.

```
<div style="width:400px; border:dotted blue;background: white">
.
.
.
</div>
```

This div is the container for the 'maximum' text box and the 'primestable' table.

```
<b>Maximum</b> <input id="maximum" value="20" /><input type="button" value="Find Primes..." onclick="findprimes();" /><br />
```

This code displays the text 'Maximum' in bold and renders a input text box which says 'Find Primes...' and on being clicked calls the 'findprimes();' function.

```
<table id="primestable">
  <tr>
    <th>Primes</th>
  </tr>
</table>
```

The above snippet renders a table which is meant to display prime numbers. It has a header called 'Primes'. Its contents will be created dynamically using results from the worker.

```
<b>Last Message From Worker</b><br />
<div id="message" style="width:400px; height:50px; border:dotted blue;background: white"></div><br />
```

The above renders a label and div to display the last message from the worker. Which will be the last found prime number. We can use this for debugging purposes.

```
<b>Last Worker Error</b><br />
<div id="error" style="width:400px; height:50px; border:dotted blue;background: white"></div><br />
```

This code displays the label and div which will contain the last worker error.

Now let's create the web worker js file named 'prime-finder-web-worker.js' with the following contents.

prime-finder-web-worker.js Code

```
//importScripts('json2.js');

var max;
```

```
onmessage = function (e) {
  // starting the web worker
  max = e.data;

  findPrimes();
};
function findPrimes() {
  search: for (var n = 2; n<=max; n+=1) {
    for (var i = 2; i <= Math.sqrt(n); i += 1)
      if (n % i == 0)
        continue search;
    // found a prime!
    postMessage('<tr><td style="border:solid red;background: white">'+n+'</td></tr>');
  }

}
```

```
//importScripts('json2.js');
```

This commented statement is an example of how supporting javascripts can be imported for use by the web worker. Most Javascript libraries like JQuery, Json etc. don't work in the web worker restricted environment as they depend on the document object being present and simply throw errors and refuse to run. But if you have created something on your own you can use it in your web worker.

```
var max;
```

This variable stores the maximum number which is the ceiling below which we have to find all prime numbers.

```
onmessage = function (e) {
  // starting the web worker
  max = e.data;

  findPrimes();
};
```

This function is hooked as the event handler for the workers 'onmessage' event. Any event posted by the web page will be received by this event handler. The only message we are sending from the web page is the maximum number below which we expect the worker to return all prime numbers. So this method stores the maximum value it gets from the event data. And then calls the findPrimes() function.

```
function findPrimes() {
   search: for (var n = 2; n<=max; n+=1) {
     for (var i = 2; i <= Math.sqrt(n); i += 1)
       if (n % i == 0)
          continue search;
     // found a prime!
     postMessage('<tr><td style="border:solid red;background: white">'+n+'</td></tr>');
   }

}
```

This is the findPrimes function which is the heart of our prime number generation algorithm embedded in the web worker. It is very crude and unoptimized way to generate primes but that is not our prime motive here but rather to show how the web worker is created.

It has two nested loops. The outer one goes from 2 to maximum value. And the inner loop goes from 2 to square root of the outer loop value. If the outer loop value (the number we are testing for primeness) is divisible by the inner loop value then it is not prime and we skip it. After the inner loop completes with no possible divisions a message is posted back to the web page with a string containing the table row which will be appended to the 'primestable' table. This row contains the prime number, styles and some table row/column tags.

We are all set. Let's see this in action in various browsers. We will be entering 30 as the maximum value and hitting the 'Find Primes…' button.

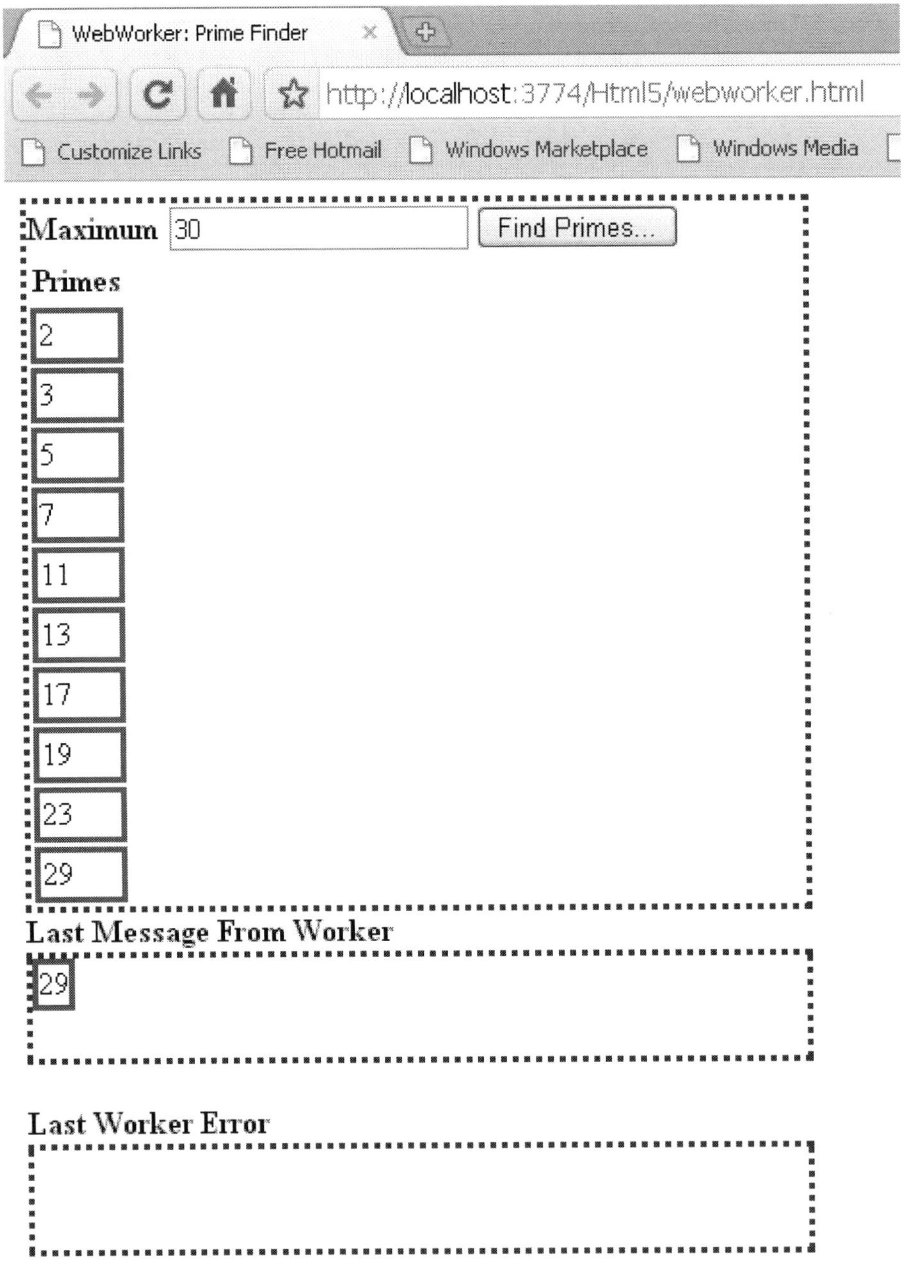

Figure 101 - Web Worker Works in Chrome

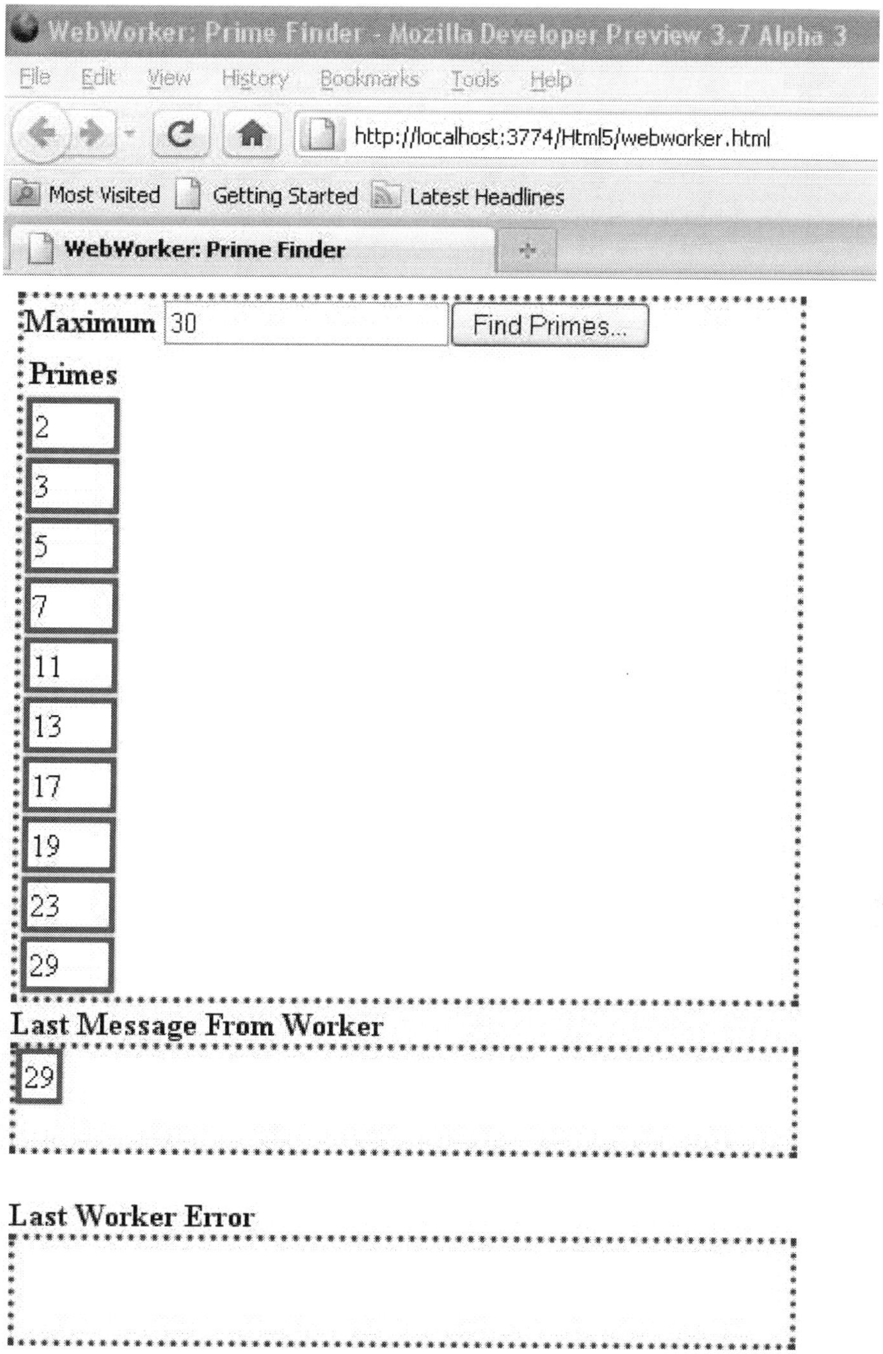

Figure 102 - Web Worker Works in Firefox

Figure 103 - Web Worker Doesn't Work in IE

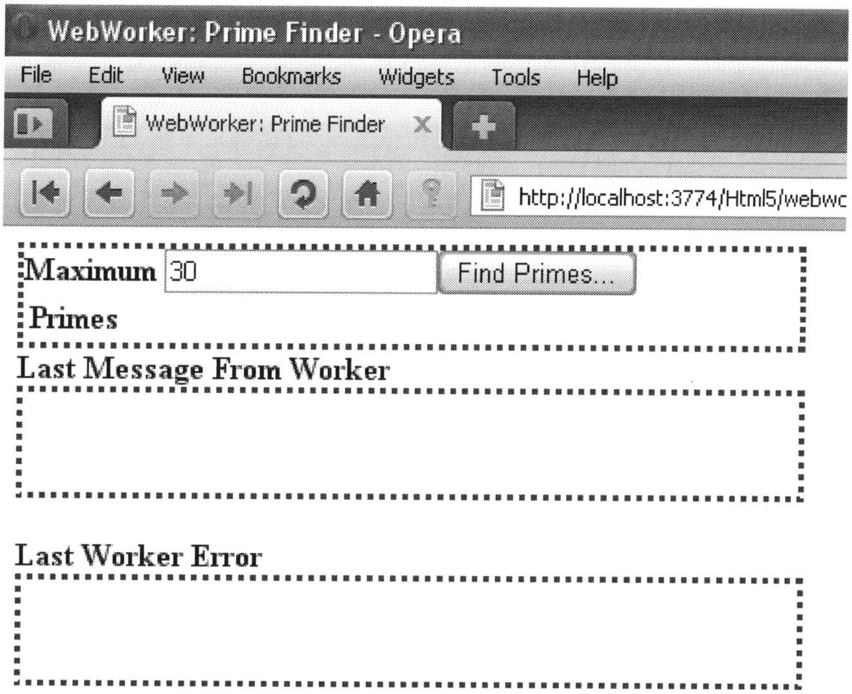

Figure 104 - Web Worker Doesn't Work in Opera

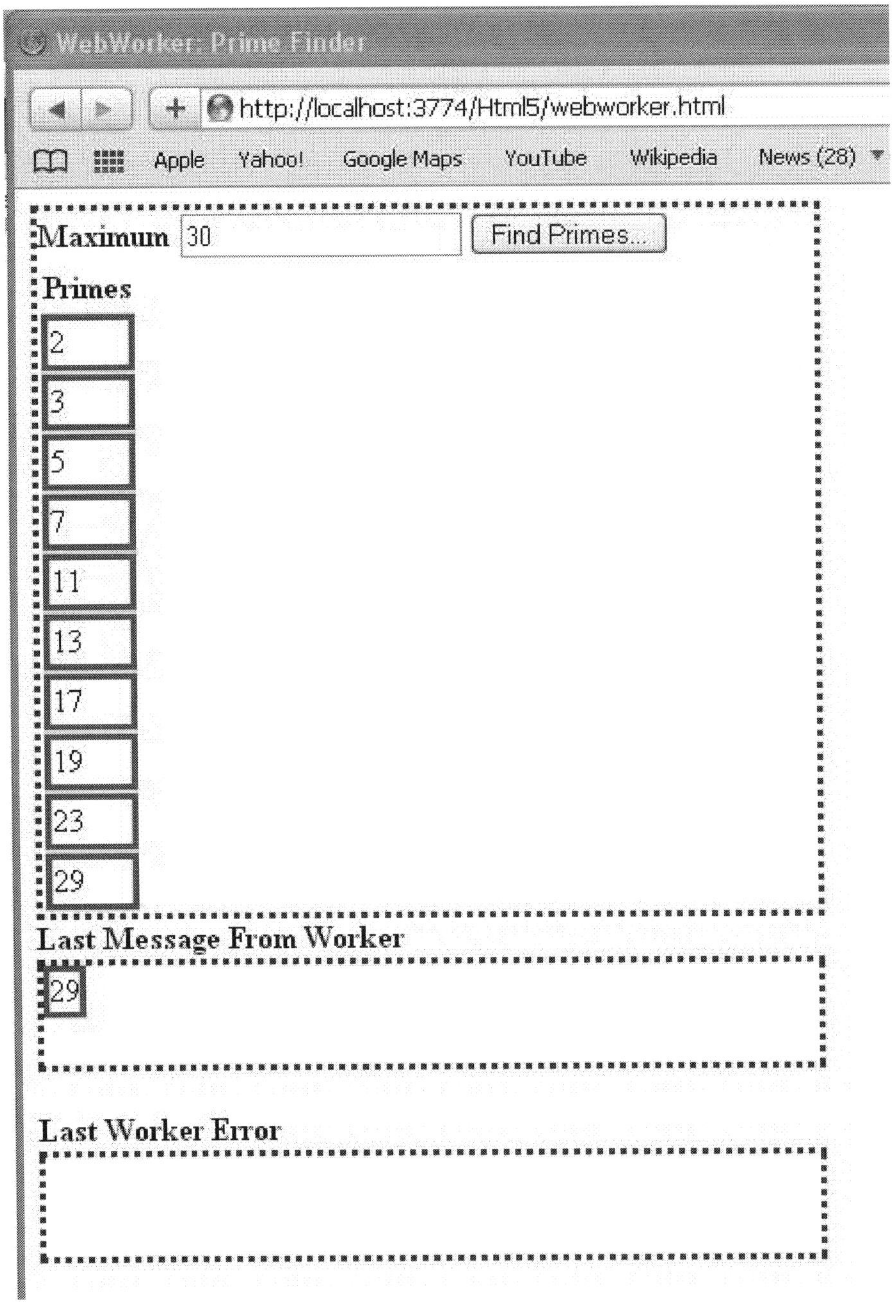

Figure 105 - Web Worker Works in Safari

A Quick Walkthrough of the Specifications

The simplest use for a worker is to perform a computationally intensive task without interrupting the user interface.

```
var worker = new Worker('worker.js');

worker.onmessage = function (event) {
    document.getElementById('result').textContent = event.data;
};
```

The first line initializes a worker and then the code uses the onmessage event handler to receive messages from the worker. It can post messages to the worker using

```
worker.postMessage('Message to the worker');
```

```
importScripts('io.js');
```

importScripts(...) can be used in a worker to import another javascript library for its use.

A Shared worker uses a slightly different syntax based on messaging channels for communication as follows

```
<script>
 var worker = new SharedWorker('test.js');
 var log = document.getElementById('log');
 worker.port.onmessage = function(e) { // note: not worker.onmessage!
   log.textContent += '\n' + e.data;
 }

 worker.port.postMessage('Message to the worker');
</script>
```

```
worker.port.addEventListener('message', function(e) {
    log.textContent += '\n' + e.data;
  }, false);
  worker.port.start(); // note: need this when using addEventListener
```

The SharedWorker is constructed using new SharedWorker(…);

If you are using .addEventListener to hook onto the message event then you have to say worker.port.start();

And the worker itself uses the following to communicate.

```
onconnect = function(e) {
  var port = e.ports[0];
  port.postMessage('Hello World!');
}
```

The worker uses the onconnect event handler to store a reference to the port corresponding to one page messaging it. And then it can use the port to post messages and hook onto the ports onmessage event handler to receive messages. This allows multiple connections to be open to the SharedWorker.

```
port.onmessage = function(e) {
    port.postMessage('pong'); // not e.ports[0].postMessage!
    // e.target.postMessage('pong'); would work also
}
```

The other page can also use the shared worker starting with

```
var worker = new SharedWorker('test.js');
```

And then sending messages to it and receiving messages using port's onmessage events.

Retrospective

We created a simple worker (non-shared) in this chapter to calculate prime numbers. We leave it to the readers to try out the shared worker feature on their own.

Chapter 13- Web Sockets

While there are quite a few WebSocket servers available we have chosen Netty to showcase assembling a custom server. And Jetty which is a prevalent standards based Servlet container which also supports WebSocket protocols.

Building a Multiplication WebSocket Server with Netty

Netty is a server framework using java.nio it is speculated that one netty instance can theoretically support upto 1,00,000 connections. The explanation of Netty is beyond the scope of this book. We will be assembling a multiplication WebSocket Server using Netty and JDK1.6 in this chapter. The concept for the example is very simple the client in our case an html page will open a websocket connection to the server and send a user entered integer number to it. The server will square the number and send it back which will be displayed on the browser.

We will be referring to the lone Netty jar and will create 3 classes in an eclipse command line java project. Let's create the classes one by one.

WebSocketServer.java Code

```java
package com.ayna;

import java.net.InetSocketAddress;
import java.util.concurrent.Executors;

import org.jboss.netty.bootstrap.ServerBootstrap;
import org.jboss.netty.channel.socket.nio.NioServerSocketChannelFactory;

/**
 * An HTTP server which serves Web Socket requests at:
 *
 *    http://localhost:9000/websocket
 *
 */
public class WebSocketServer {
    public static void main(String[] args) {
```

```java
        int port = 9000;

    // Configure the server.
    ServerBootstrap bootstrap = new ServerBootstrap(
        new NioServerSocketChannelFactory(
            Executors.newCachedThreadPool(),
            Executors.newCachedThreadPool()));

    // Set up the event pipeline factory.
    bootstrap.setPipelineFactory(new WebSocketServerPipelineFactory());

    // Bind and start to accept incoming connections.
    bootstrap.bind(new InetSocketAddress(port));

    System.out.println("WebSocket Server Started");
    System.out.println("WebSocket Accessible on
http://localhost:"+port+WebSocketServerHandler.WEBSOCKET_PATH);
    }
}
```

This is the main class. It will start a WebSocket server accessible on http://localhost:9000/websocket . Usually to make things secure we should implement same-origin constraints in the client-server web application, which means only those pages which are loaded from the same origin as the websocket server can call the websocket server. In this example we have not implemented any such mechanism so this server should ideally not be used as is for internet applications but rather intranet/enterprise applications.

WebSocketServerHandler.java Code

```java
package com.ayna;


import static org.jboss.netty.handler.codec.http.HttpHeaders.*;
import static org.jboss.netty.handler.codec.http.HttpHeaders.Names.*;
import static org.jboss.netty.handler.codec.http.HttpHeaders.Values.*;
import static org.jboss.netty.handler.codec.http.HttpMethod.*;
import static org.jboss.netty.handler.codec.http.HttpResponseStatus.*;
import static org.jboss.netty.handler.codec.http.HttpVersion.*;

import org.jboss.netty.buffer.ChannelBuffer;
import org.jboss.netty.buffer.ChannelBuffers;
import org.jboss.netty.channel.ChannelFuture;
```

```java
import org.jboss.netty.channel.ChannelFutureListener;
import org.jboss.netty.channel.ChannelHandlerContext;
import org.jboss.netty.channel.ChannelPipeline;
import org.jboss.netty.channel.ExceptionEvent;
import org.jboss.netty.channel.MessageEvent;
import org.jboss.netty.channel.SimpleChannelUpstreamHandler;
import org.jboss.netty.handler.codec.http.DefaultHttpResponse;
import org.jboss.netty.handler.codec.http.HttpHeaders;
import org.jboss.netty.handler.codec.http.HttpRequest;
import org.jboss.netty.handler.codec.http.HttpResponse;
import org.jboss.netty.handler.codec.http.HttpResponseStatus;
import org.jboss.netty.handler.codec.http.HttpHeaders.Names;
import org.jboss.netty.handler.codec.http.HttpHeaders.Values;
import org.jboss.netty.handler.codec.http.websocket.DefaultWebSocketFrame;
import org.jboss.netty.handler.codec.http.websocket.WebSocketFrame;
import org.jboss.netty.handler.codec.http.websocket.WebSocketFrameDecoder;
import org.jboss.netty.handler.codec.http.websocket.WebSocketFrameEncoder;
import org.jboss.netty.util.CharsetUtil;


public class WebSocketServerHandler extends SimpleChannelUpstreamHandler {

  public static final String WEBSOCKET_PATH = "/websocket";

  @Override
  public void messageReceived(ChannelHandlerContext ctx, MessageEvent e) throws Exception {
    Object msg = e.getMessage();
    if (msg instanceof HttpRequest) {
      handleHttpRequest(ctx, (HttpRequest) msg);
    } else if (msg instanceof WebSocketFrame) {
      handleWebSocketFrame(ctx, (WebSocketFrame) msg);
    }
  }

  private void handleHttpRequest(ChannelHandlerContext ctx, HttpRequest req) {
    // Allow only GET methods.
    if (req.getMethod() != GET) {
      sendHttpResponse(
          ctx, req, new DefaultHttpResponse(HTTP_1_1, FORBIDDEN));
      return;
    }

    // Serve the WebSocket handshake request.
    if (req.getUri().equals(WEBSOCKET_PATH) &&
        Values.UPGRADE.equalsIgnoreCase(req.getHeader(CONNECTION)) &&
        WEBSOCKET.equalsIgnoreCase(req.getHeader(Names.UPGRADE))) {

      // Create the WebSocket handshake response.
      HttpResponse res = new DefaultHttpResponse(
          HTTP_1_1,
          new HttpResponseStatus(101, "Web Socket Protocol Handshake"));
      res.addHeader(Names.UPGRADE, WEBSOCKET);
      res.addHeader(CONNECTION, Values.UPGRADE);
      res.addHeader(WEBSOCKET_ORIGIN, req.getHeader(ORIGIN));
      res.addHeader(WEBSOCKET_LOCATION, getWebSocketLocation(req));
```

```
        String protocol = req.getHeader(WEBSOCKET_PROTOCOL);
        if (protocol != null) {
           res.addHeader(WEBSOCKET_PROTOCOL, protocol);
        }

        // Upgrade the connection and send the handshake response.
        ChannelPipeline p = ctx.getChannel().getPipeline();
        p.remove("aggregator");
        p.replace("decoder", "wsdecoder", new WebSocketFrameDecoder());

        ctx.getChannel().write(res);

        p.replace("encoder", "wsencoder", new WebSocketFrameEncoder());
        return;
     }

     // Send an error page otherwise.
     sendHttpResponse(
        ctx, req, new DefaultHttpResponse(HTTP_1_1, FORBIDDEN));
  }

  /*
   * This is the meat of the server event processing
   * Here we square the number and return it
   */
  private void handleWebSocketFrame(ChannelHandlerContext ctx, WebSocketFrame frame) {
        System.out.println(frame.getTextData());
        int number = 0;
        try {
                number = Integer.parseInt(frame.getTextData());

        } catch (Exception e){
                System.out.println("Invalid Number: Parsing Exception.");
        }
        //Square the number
        int result = number * number;

     // Send the square of the number back.
     ctx.getChannel().write(
        new DefaultWebSocketFrame(result+""));
  }

  private void sendHttpResponse(ChannelHandlerContext ctx, HttpRequest req, HttpResponse res)
{
     // Generate an error page if response status code is not OK (200).
     if (res.getStatus().getCode() != 200) {
       res.setContent(
          ChannelBuffers.copiedBuffer(
               res.getStatus().toString(), CharsetUtil.UTF_8));
       setContentLength(res, res.getContent().readableBytes());
     }

     // Send the response and close the connection if necessary.
     ChannelFuture f = ctx.getChannel().write(res);
     if (!isKeepAlive(req) || res.getStatus().getCode() != 200) {
```

```
        f.addListener(ChannelFutureListener.CLOSE);
    }
  }

  @Override
  public void exceptionCaught(ChannelHandlerContext ctx, ExceptionEvent e)
      throws Exception {
    e.getCause().printStackTrace();
    e.getChannel().close();
  }

  private String getWebSocketLocation(HttpRequest req) {
    return "ws://" + req.getHeader(HttpHeaders.Names.HOST) + WEBSOCKET_PATH;
  }
}
```

While we will not make an attempt to explain the code in this class the following code is the meat of this class i.e. the core business functionality of the server which is multiplication of integer numbers.

```
private void handleWebSocketFrame(ChannelHandlerContext ctx, WebSocketFrame frame) {
        System.out.println(frame.getTextData());
        int number = 0;
        try {
                number = Integer.parseInt(frame.getTextData());

        } catch (Exception e){
                System.out.println("Invalid Number: Parsing Exception.");
        }
        //Square the number
        int result = number * number;

      // Send the square of the number back.
      ctx.getChannel().write(
          new DefaultWebSocketFrame(result+""));
  }
```

This method handles the web socket frame. The number sent by the client is retrieved through 'frame.getTextData()' it parsed and squared and then sent back to the client using 'ctx.getChannel().write(new DefaultWebSocketFrame(result + ""));'

WebSocketServerPipelineFactory.java Code
package **com.ayna**;

```java
import static org.jboss.netty.channel.Channels.*;

import org.jboss.netty.channel.ChannelPipeline;
import org.jboss.netty.channel.ChannelPipelineFactory;
import org.jboss.netty.handler.codec.http.HttpChunkAggregator;
import org.jboss.netty.handler.codec.http.HttpRequestDecoder;
import org.jboss.netty.handler.codec.http.HttpResponseEncoder;


public class WebSocketServerPipelineFactory implements ChannelPipelineFactory {
    public ChannelPipeline getPipeline() throws Exception {
        // Create a default pipeline implementation.
        ChannelPipeline pipeline = pipeline();
        pipeline.addLast("decoder", new HttpRequestDecoder());
        pipeline.addLast("aggregator", new HttpChunkAggregator(65536));
        pipeline.addLast("encoder", new HttpResponseEncoder());
        pipeline.addLast("handler", new WebSocketServerHandler());
        return pipeline;
    }
}
```

We will not attempt to explain this class but rather point you to the Netty documentation at http://www.jboss.org/netty/documentation.html for self reading.

Let's build the client side html page.

index.html Code

```html
<!DOCTYPE html>
<!-- Tested In Chrome. -->
<html>
<head>
<meta http-equiv="Content-Type" content="text/html; charset=ISO-8859-1">
<title>WebSocket: Squaring Service</title>
  <script type="text/javascript" charset="utf-8" src="js/jquery-1.3.2.js"></script>

  <script type="text/javascript">
    var ws;

    $(document).ready(function () {
      ws = new WebSocket("ws://localhost:9000/websocket");
      ws.onopen = function(event) { $('#status').text("The WebSocket Connection Is Open."); }
                    ws.onmessage = function(event) { $('#result').text("Result= "+event.data); }
                    ws.onclose = function(event) { $('#status').text("The WebSocket Connection
Has Been Closed."); }

    });

    function sendNumber(){
```

```
            var number = $('#number').val();
            ws.send(number);
        }

    </script>
</head>
<body>
    <h1>WebSocket: Squaring Service</h1>
    <div id="status"></div><br/>
    Enter The Number To Square <input id="number" value="10"/><input type="button"
value="Square It..." onclick="sendNumber();" /><br/>
    <div id="result"></div><br/>
</body>
</html>
```

```
<div id="status"></div><br/>
```

The above div will report the status of the connection.

```
Enter The Number To Square <input id="number" value="10"/><input type="button" value="Square It..."
onclick="sendNumber();" /><br/>
```

The above code renders the label 'Enter The Number To Square' followed by an input text box with the id 'number' and then a button with the label 'Square It...' which on being clicked will call the 'sendNumber' method.

```
<div id="result"></div><br/>
```

The above div will be used to display the result returned from the WebSocket server. It will be the square of the number entered by the user.

```
<script type="text/javascript" charset="utf-8" src="js/jquery-1.3.2.js"></script>
```

This page uses the JQuery javascript library.

```
var ws;
```

the 'ws' variable will be used to store a reference to the WebSocket.

```
$(document).ready(function () {
    ws = new WebSocket("ws://localhost:9000/websocket");
    ws.onopen = function(event) { $('#status').text("The WebSocket Connection Is Open."); }
    ws.onmessage = function(event) { $('#result').text("Result= "+event.data); }
    ws.onclose = function(event) { $('#status').text("The WebSocket Connection Has Been Closed."); }

});
```

This statement calls the inline function when the document is ready. The inline function opens a new WebSocket to the 'ws://localhost:9000/websocket' url. Then it hooks 3 functions one each to the 'open', 'message' and 'close' events. The 'open' and 'close' event handlers are called when the WebSocket connection is opened and closed respectively, and the handlers update the status in the div with the id as 'status'. The 'message' event handler will be called when a message is received from the server and it displays the result in the div with the id 'result'.

```
function sendNumber(){
    var number = $('#number').val();
    ws.send(number);
}
```

The above function gets called when the 'Square It…' buttons is clicked by the user after he enters an integer number. This function retrieves the number from the text box with the id 'number' and then calls the websocket 'send' method to send the number to the websocket.

We are all set. Start the WebSocketServer, it will display the following

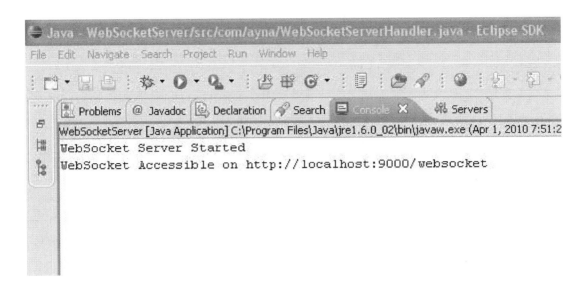

Figure 106 - Netty WebSocket Server Console Output

Double click the index.html file and open it in Chrome browser. Enter an integer number in the text box e.g. 12 and hit the 'Square It...' button. The page will make the call to the server and display the result it receives from the server i.e. 144 as shown below.

WebSocket: Squaring Service

The WebSocket Connection Is Open.

Enter The Number To Square 12   Square It...
Result= 144

Figure 107 - The Netty WebSocket Server Squares 12 and Returns 144

Building a Chat Application over a WebSocket Server using Jetty 7.0.1

Let's create a chat application using Jetty. Create a dynamic web application project in Eclipse and create the following class.

```
WebSocketChatServlet.java Code

package com.ayna;

import java.io.IOException;
import java.util.Set;
import java.util.concurrent.CopyOnWriteArraySet;

import javax.servlet.ServletException;
import javax.servlet.http.HttpServletRequest;
import javax.servlet.http.HttpServletResponse;

import org.eclipse.jetty.websocket.WebSocket;
import org.eclipse.jetty.websocket.WebSocketConnection;
import org.eclipse.jetty.websocket.WebSocketServlet;

public class WebSocketChatServlet extends WebSocketServlet
{
    private final Set<ChatWebSocket> users = new CopyOnWriteArraySet();

    protected void doGet(HttpServletRequest request, HttpServletResponse response)
        throws ServletException ,IOException
    {
        getServletContext().getNamedDispatcher("default").forward(request,response);
    }

    protected WebSocket doWebSocketConnect(HttpServletRequest request, String protocol)
    {
        return new ChatWebSocket();
    }

    class ChatWebSocket implements WebSocket
    {
        WebSocketConnection connection;

        public void onConnect(Outbound connection)
        {
            ChatWebSocket.this.connection= (WebSocketConnection) connection;
            users.add(this);
        }

        public void onMessage(byte frame, byte[] data,int offset, int length)
        {
            // binary communication not needed
        }

        public void onMessage(byte frame, String data)
```

```
    {
        for (ChatWebSocket user : users)
        {
            try
            {
                user.connection.sendMessage(frame,data);
            }
            catch(Exception e) {}
        }
    }
    public void onDisconnect()
    {
        users.remove(this);
    }
  }
}
```

The WebSocketServlet is the base class which provides the WebSocket feature. The doGet method responds to a HTTP GET request which is when the WebSocket handshake happens. It then upgrades the protocol to WebSocket protocol this is when the doWebsocketConnect happens. The ChatWebSocket class is the heart of the businesslogic and it is also used to store a reference to the connection. A 'users' stores all the WebSockets. The WebSocket supports two kinds of content Text and Binary. For our purpose we are not using any binary payload so the method

```
public void onMessage(byte frame, byte[] data,int offset, int length)
```

is empty. The following method gets called when a Text message is received from Any chat user.

```
public void onMessage(byte frame, String data)
```

The method then loops over all the WebSockets and broadcasts the incoming message to all of them hence creating a chat like application.

The web.xml file is as follows.

web.xml content

```xml
<?xml version="1.0" encoding="UTF-8"?>
<web-app id="WebApp_ID" version="2.4"
xmlns="http://java.sun.com/xml/ns/j2ee"
xmlns:xsi="http://www.w3.org/2001/XMLSchema-instance"
xsi:schemaLocation="http://java.sun.com/xml/ns/j2ee
http://java.sun.com/xml/ns/j2ee/web-app_2_4.xsd">
        <display-name>ChatWebSocketServer</display-name>

    <servlet>
        <servlet-name>WebSocketChat</servlet-name>
        <servlet-class>com.ayna.WebSocketChatServlet</servlet-class>
        <load-on-startup>1</load-on-startup>
    </servlet>

    <servlet-mapping>
            <servlet-name>WebSocketChat</servlet-name>
    <url-pattern>/wsc/*</url-pattern>
    </servlet-mapping>

    <welcome-file-list>
        <welcome-file>index.html</welcome-file>
        <welcome-file>index.htm</welcome-file>
        <welcome-file>index.jsp</welcome-file>
        <welcome-file>default.html</welcome-file>
        <welcome-file>default.htm</welcome-file>
        <welcome-file>default.jsp</welcome-file>
    </welcome-file-list>
</web-app>
```

The above web.xml file configures the WebSocket Servlet. Let's create the chat front end html file as follows.

index.html Code

```html
<!DOCTYPE html>
<!-- Tested In Chrome. -->
<html>
<head>
<meta http-equiv="Content-Type" content="text/html; charset=ISO-8859-1">
```

```html
<title>WebSocket: Chat </title>
  <script type="text/javascript" charset="utf-8" src="js/jquery-1.3.2.js"></script>

  <script type="text/javascript">
    var ws;

    $(document).ready(function () {
        var loc = window.location;
        var host = loc.host;
        ws = new WebSocket("ws://"+host+"/ChatWebSocketServer/wsc/anything");
        ws.onopen = function(event) { $('#status').text("The Chat Connection Is Open."); }
        ws.onmessage = function(event) {
            var $textarea = $('#messages');
            $textarea.val( $textarea.val() + event.data+"\n");
            $textarea.animate({ scrollTop: $textarea.height() }, 1000);
        }
        ws.onclose = function(event) { $('#status').text("The Chat Connection Has Been Closed."); }
    });

    function sendMessage(){
        var message = $('#username').val()+":"+$('#message').val();
        ws.send(message);
        $('#message').val(");
    }

  </script>
</head>
<body>
  <h1>WebSocket: Chat</h1>
  <div id="status"></div><br/>
  Username <input id="username" value="anonymous"/><br/>
  <textarea id="messages" rows="20" cols="60" readonly="readonly" ></textarea><br/>
  <input id="message" type="text"/><input type="button" value="Send..."
onclick="sendMessage();"/></br>

</body>
</html>
```

We are using the JQuery Javascript library in this application.

```
var ws;
```

This variable is used to store the reference to the WebSocket.

```
$(document).ready(function () {
        var loc = window.location;
        var host = loc.host;
        ws = new WebSocket("ws://"+host+"/ChatWebSocketServer/wsc/anything");
```

```
ws.onopen = function(event) { $('#status').text("The Chat Connection Is Open."); }
ws.onmessage = function(event) {
    var $textarea = $('#messages');
    $textarea.val( $textarea.val() + event.data+"\n");
    $textarea.animate({ scrollTop: $textarea.height() }, 1000);
}
ws.onclose = function(event) { $('#status').text("The Chat Connection Has Been Closed."); }
});
```

The above code links the inline function to the document ready event. The inline function retrieves the 'host' string from the url which in our case should be 'localhost:9000' as we have configured the Jetty server to start on port 9000. It then opens a WebSocket to 'ws://localhost:9000/ChatWebSocketServer/wsc/anything' ChatWebSocketServer is the context path of the web application and the Chat WebSocket Servlet is mapped to /wsc/* and hence the /wsc/anything part of the url.

The 'open' and 'close' event handlers are used to update the connection status in the status div.

The onmessage event handler adds the chat message received to the textarea and scrolls the textarea down to the maximum.

```
function sendMessage(){
    var message = $('#username').val()+":"+$('#message').val();
    ws.send(message);
    $('#message').val('');
}
```

The above function gets called when the 'Send…' button is clicked and it sends the chat message to the Chat WebSocket Server. The message is a text message of the following format '<username>:<message>' where the username is retrieved from the username text box which the user can change at anytime.

```
<div id="status"></div><br/>
```

The above div is used to display the connection status.

Username <input id="username" value="anonymous"/>

The above line renders the 'Username' label and a textbox with the id 'username' which can be used by the chat user to enter his chat alias. There is no validation or authentication in the system. And there is only one chat room i.e. if you are connected to the server you are in the chatroom.

<input id="message" type="text"/><input type="button" value="Send..." onclick="sendMessage();"/></br>

The above line renders a text box with the id 'message' which the user can use to enter his chat message into. It also renders a button with the label 'Send...' which when clicked calls the sendMessage function which will send the message to the server.

Let's take it for a spin. Deploy the web application into the webapps folder of the jetty installation. The source code bundle contains a preconfigured Jetty 7.0.1 server with the web application pre-installed (which is the minimum version of Jetty which supports the WebSocket feature)

If JDK 1.6 is installed on your system and the JAVA_HOME and PATH configured properly you can double click start.jar in the jetty folder to run the server. Or you can type 'java –jar start.jar' from the command line in the Jetty folder.

Launch two browser tabs and open the following URL in both http://localhost:9000/ChatWebSocketServer/

Enter different chat aliases in both the tabs and wait for the connection to establish. And start chatting. See below.

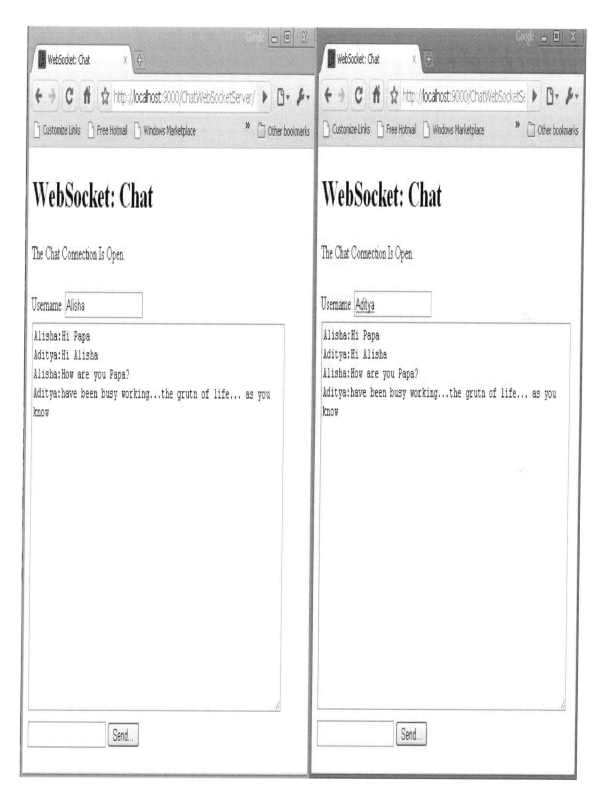

Let's try the Chat WebSocket Application in other browsers.

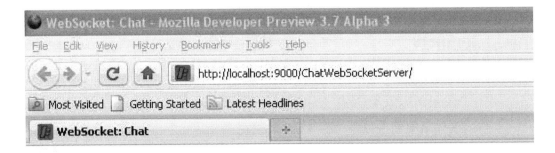

WebSocket: Chat

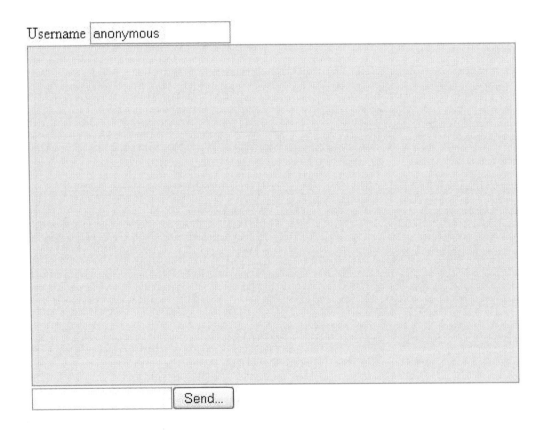

Figure 108 - WebSocket Chat Doesn't Work/Connect in Firefox

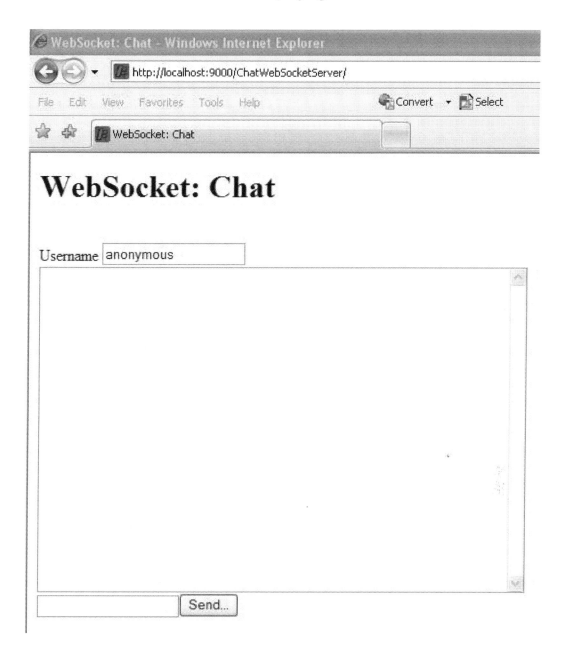

Figure 109 - WebSocket Chat Doesn't Work/Connect in IE

WebSocket: Chat

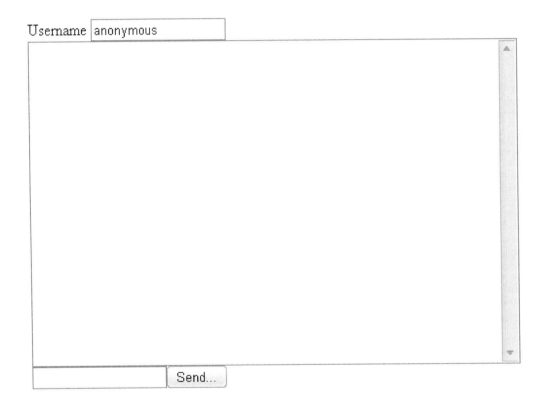

Figure 110 - WebSocket Chat Doesn't Work/Connect in Opera

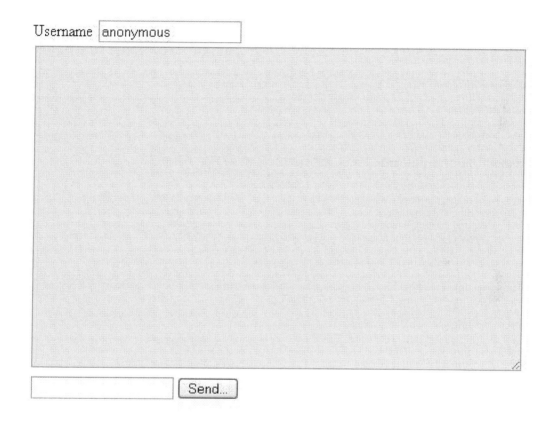

Figure 111 - WebSocket Chat Doesn't Work/Connect in Safari

A Quick Walkthrough of the Specifications

The web sockets specification is very short and simple. Web Sockets is a way of establishing a duplex communication channel with a backend server. It is different from earlier adhoc non-standard methods used by developers like

Reverse Ajax, Comet and Pushlets. Which were limited by the 2 connection browser limit. Which doesn't apply to WebSockets or Server Sent Events for that matter. But on the other hand WebSocket based applications are prone to too many connections overwhelming the server. Security over internet is provided by the application of same-origin policy between the web page and the WebSocket server.

WebSocket protocol starts with an HTTP request which then upgrades to the WebSocket protocol. The protocol is very simple and allows UTF-8 characters in text messages followed by a delimiter. And for binary messages the length is specified. Unlike HTTP it is not a request-response protocol and once the connection is established both sides can send as many messages as and when they need to send them as long as the connection is open.

There are 5 things to be done.

```
var ws = new WebSocket("ws://www.mydomain.com/endpointpath")
```

We open a new WebSocket connection to the backend server. And then we hook onto the 'open', 'message', 'error' and 'close' events.

```
ws.onopen = function(event) { alert("We are connected to the backend server"); }
```

```
ws.onmessage = function(event) { alert("Recieved: " + event.data); }
```

```
ws.onerror = function(event){ alert("error encountered"); }
```

```
ws.onclose = function(event) { alert("Connection to the backend server closed"); }
```

The open event is fired when we get connected to the backend server. The read event is fired when something is received from the backend server. And the close event is fired when the server connection is closed/lost.

```
ws.send("string message payload")
```

The send method sends a message to the server. That's all there is to it apart from the details.

The WebSocket constructor can take a protocol parameter apart from the URL 'new WebSocket(url, protocol)' The protocol parameter is a sub-protocol that the server must support for the connection to be successful. The constructor is a non-blocking call. The URL will start with 'ws://' or 'wss://', the latter is for the secure protocol.

The 'URL' attribute of a WebSocket returns the resolved URL which may or may not be the same as the URL passed in the constructor.

The 'readyState' attribute can be

- CONNECTING (numeric value 0) - The connection has not yet been established.

- OPEN (numeric value 1) - The WebSocket connection is established and communication is possible.

- CLOSING (numeric value 2) - The connection is going through the closing handshake.

- CLOSED (numeric value 3) - The connection has been closed or could not be opened.

The 'send(data)' method sends the data to the server if the state is OPEN. Else it throws an error.

The 'close' method of the websocket closes the connection. The 'bufferedAmount' attribute returns the number of bytes that have been queued but not yet sent to the server.

Retrospective

Instead of explaining WebSockets with proprietary server side software we showed how to create a simple multiplication service with a two way channel using Netty. We also created a simple chat application using the implementation of WebSockets in Jetty 7.0.1. We leave it to the readers to explore other proprietary servers available and also to explore the same origin constraints applicable in their use which will be required when creating an internet facing application.

6972007R0

Made in the USA
Lexington, KY
07 October 2010